3 0183 05010 0989

D1404107

Jackie Robinson

written by
Joe Dunn

illustrated by
Rod Espinosa

magic
Wagon

visit us at
www.abdopublishing.com

Published by Magic Wagon, a division of the ABDO Publishing Group, 8000 West 78th Street, Edina, Minnesota 55439. Copyright © 2008 by Abdo Consulting Group, Inc. International copyrights reserved in all countries. All rights reserved. No part of this book may be reproduced in any form without written permission from the publisher. Graphic Planet™ is a trademark and logo of Magic Wagon.

Printed in the United States.

Written by Joe Dunn
Illustrated by Rod Espinosa
Colored and lettered by Rod Espinosa
Edited by Stephanie Hedlund
Interior layout and design by Antarctic Press
Cover art by Rod Espinosa
Cover design by Neil Klinepier

Library of Congress Cataloging-in-Publication Data

Dunn, Joeming W.
    Jackie Robinson / written by Joe Dunn ; illustrated by Rod Espinosa.
    p. cm. -- (Bio-graphics)
    Includes index.
    ISBN-13: 978-1-60270-068-0
    1. Robinson, Jackie, 1919-1972--Juvenile literature. 2. Baseball players--United States--Biography--Juvenile literature. 3. African American baseball players--Biography--Juvenile literature. 4. Graphic novels. I. Title.

GV865.R6E85 2008
 796.357092--dc22
[B]   2007012065

TABLE of CONTENTS

Timeline

January 31, 1919 - Jackie Robinson was born in Cairo, Georgia.

September 1939 - Robinson enrolled at UCLA and became the school's first 4-letter athlete.

April 3, 1942 - Robinson was inducted into the U.S. Army.

November 28, 1944 - Robinson received an honorable discharge from the military.

August 28, 1945 - Robinson met with Branch Rickey of the Dodgers and joined the team.

October 23, 1945 - Robinson played with the Montreal Royals.

February 10, 1945 - Robinson married Rachel Isum.

April 15, 1946 - Robinson made his major league debut against the Boston Braves.

October 19, 1947 - Robinson was voted Rookie of the Year.

October 1949 - Robinson was named the National League's Most Valuable Player.

October 4, 1955 - The Dodgers won their first World Series.

January 1955 - Robinson resigned as a baseball player.

1958 - Robinson became a spokesperson for the NAACP.

January 23, 1960 - Robinson was inducted into the Baseball Hall of Fame.

October 23, 1971 - Robinson died in Stamford, Connecticut.

August 2, 1982 - Robinson became the first baseball player on a U.S. postage stamp.

1984 - Robinson was awarded the Medal of Freedom.

1997 - Robinson's number 42 was retired permanently by Major League Baseball.

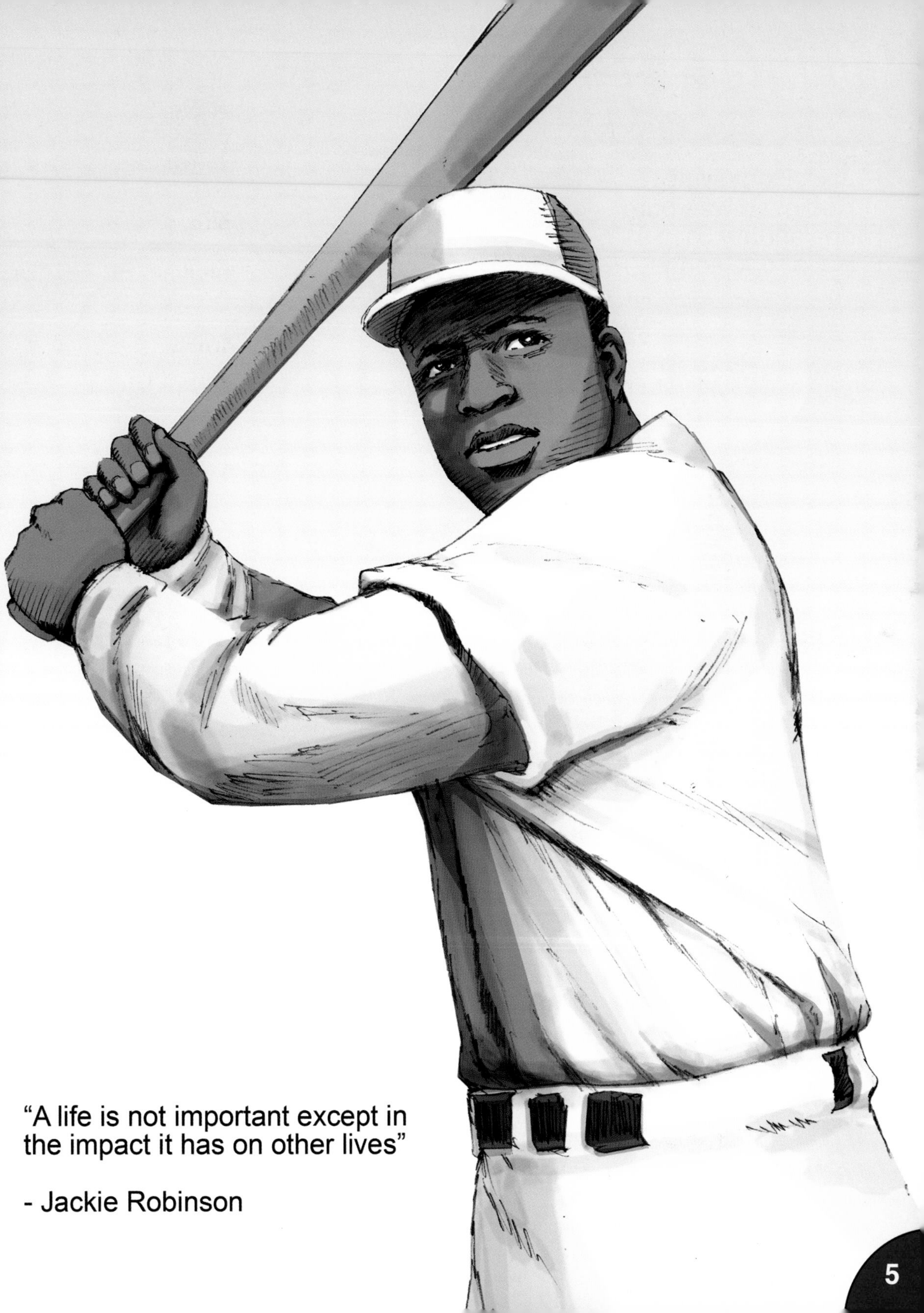

“A life is not important except in the impact it has on other lives”

- Jackie Robinson

Chapter 1 Birth and Childhood

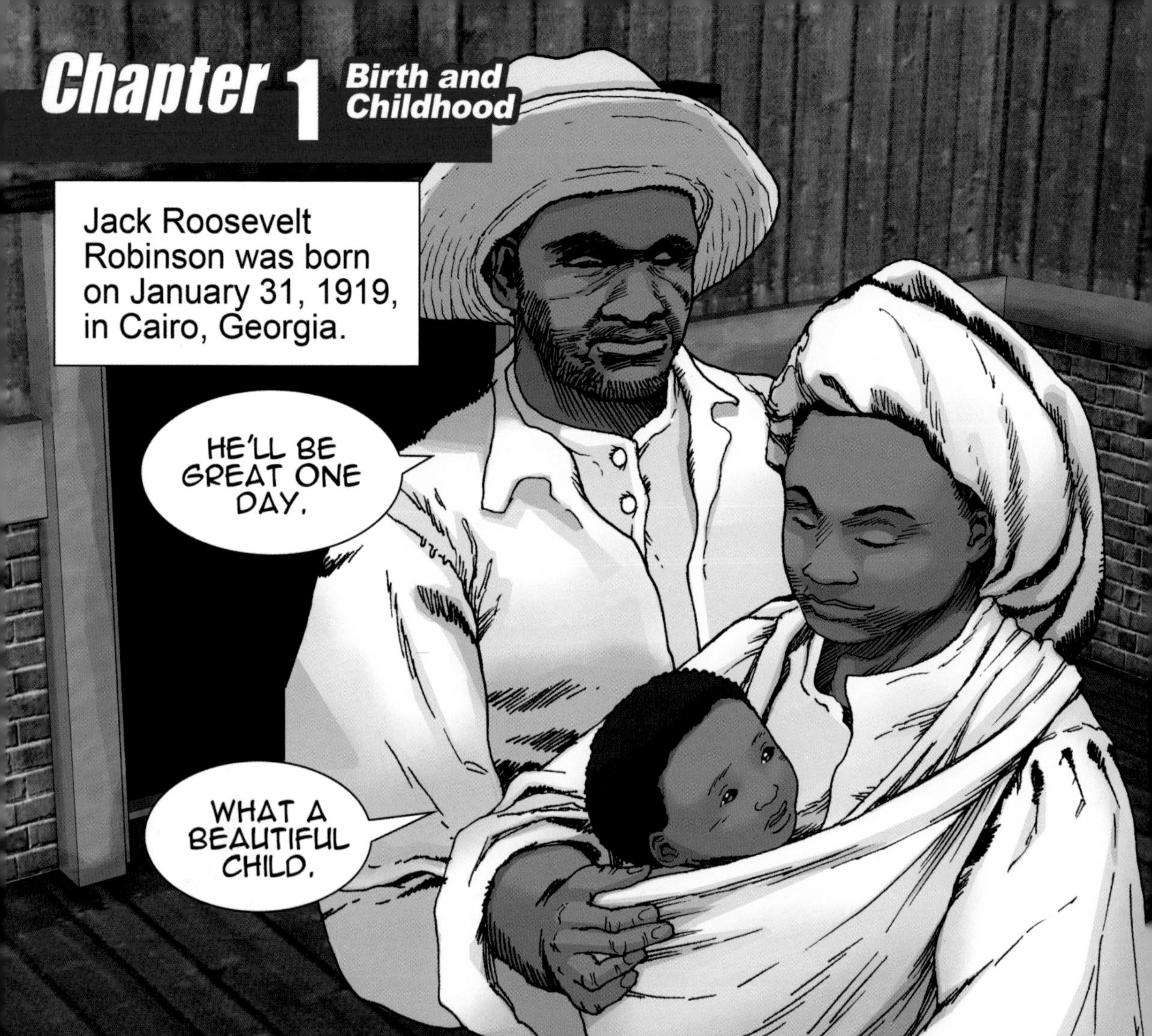
Jack Roosevelt Robinson was born on January 31, 1919, in Cairo, Georgia.
HE'LL BE GREAT ONE DAY.
WHAT A BEAUTIFUL CHILD.

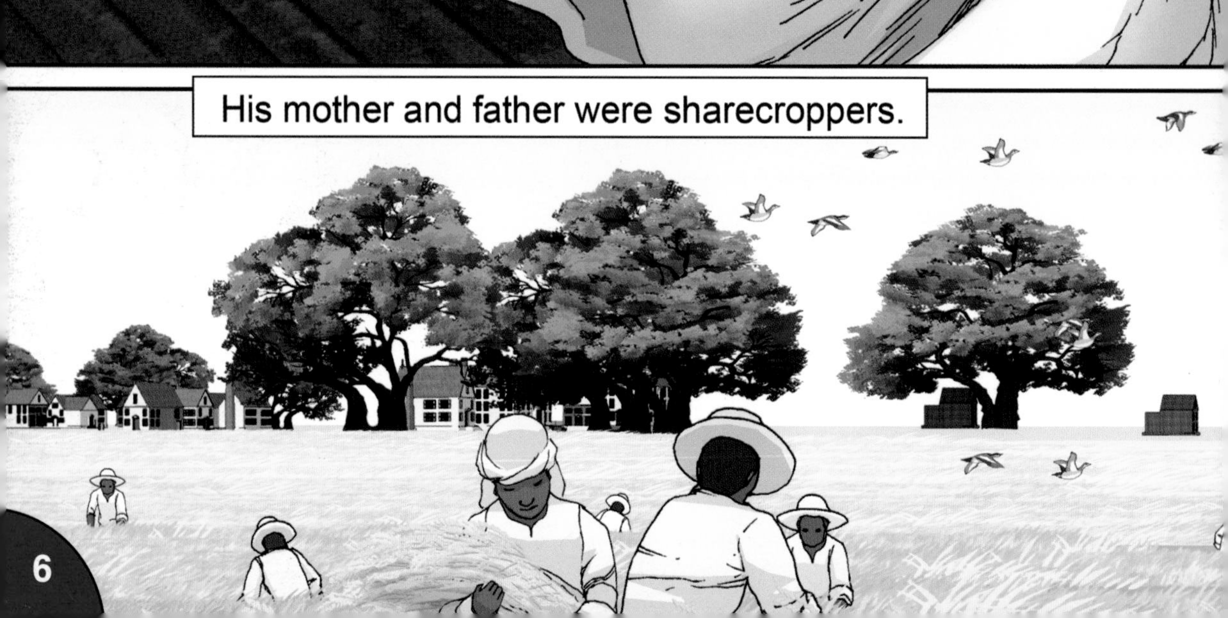
His mother and father were sharecroppers.

Jackie's father left the family. His mother, Mallie Robinson, had to raise him and his four bothers and sisters single-handedly.

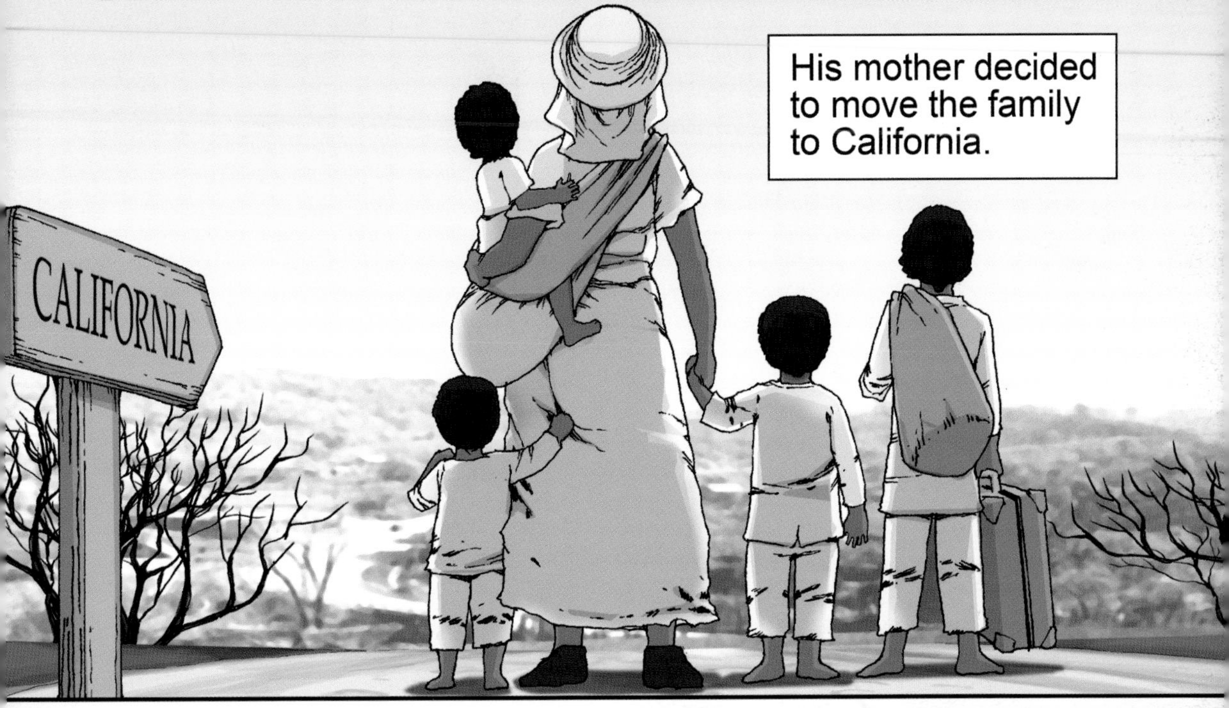
His mother decided to move the family to California.
CALIFORNIA

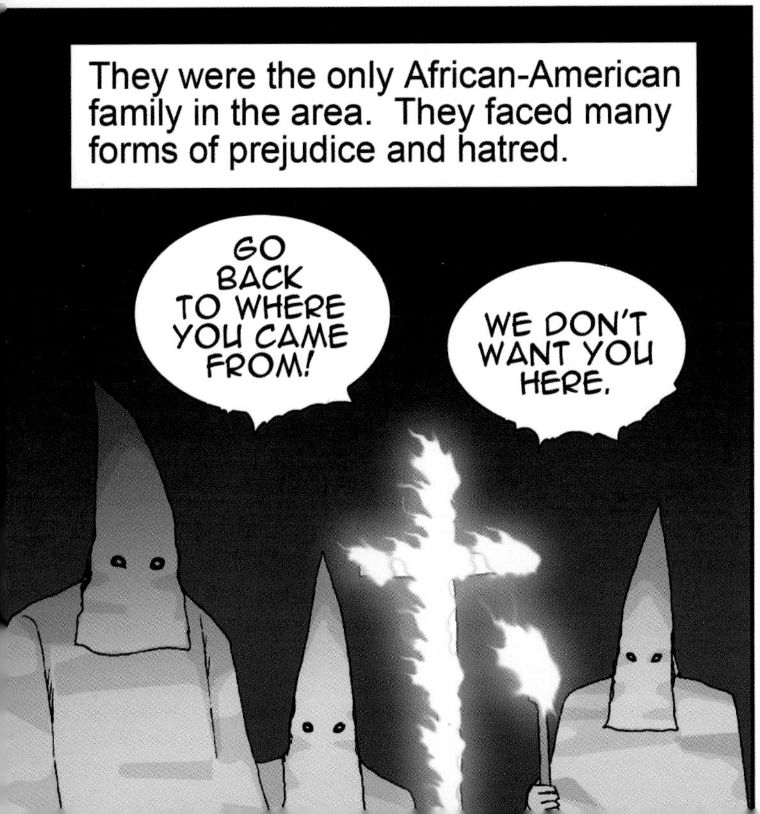
They were the only African-American family in the area. They faced many forms of prejudice and hatred.
GO BACK TO WHERE YOU CAME FROM!
WE DON'T WANT YOU HERE.

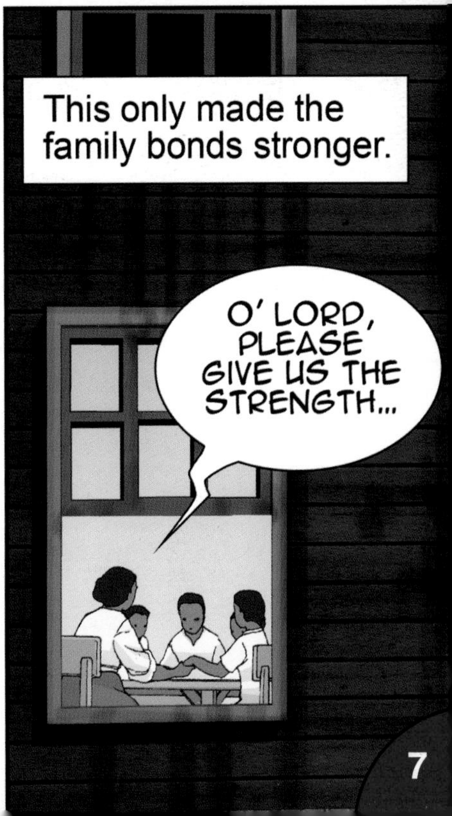
This only made the family bonds stronger.
O' LORD, PLEASE GIVE US THE STRENGTH...

Chapter 2 A Life Filled with Sports

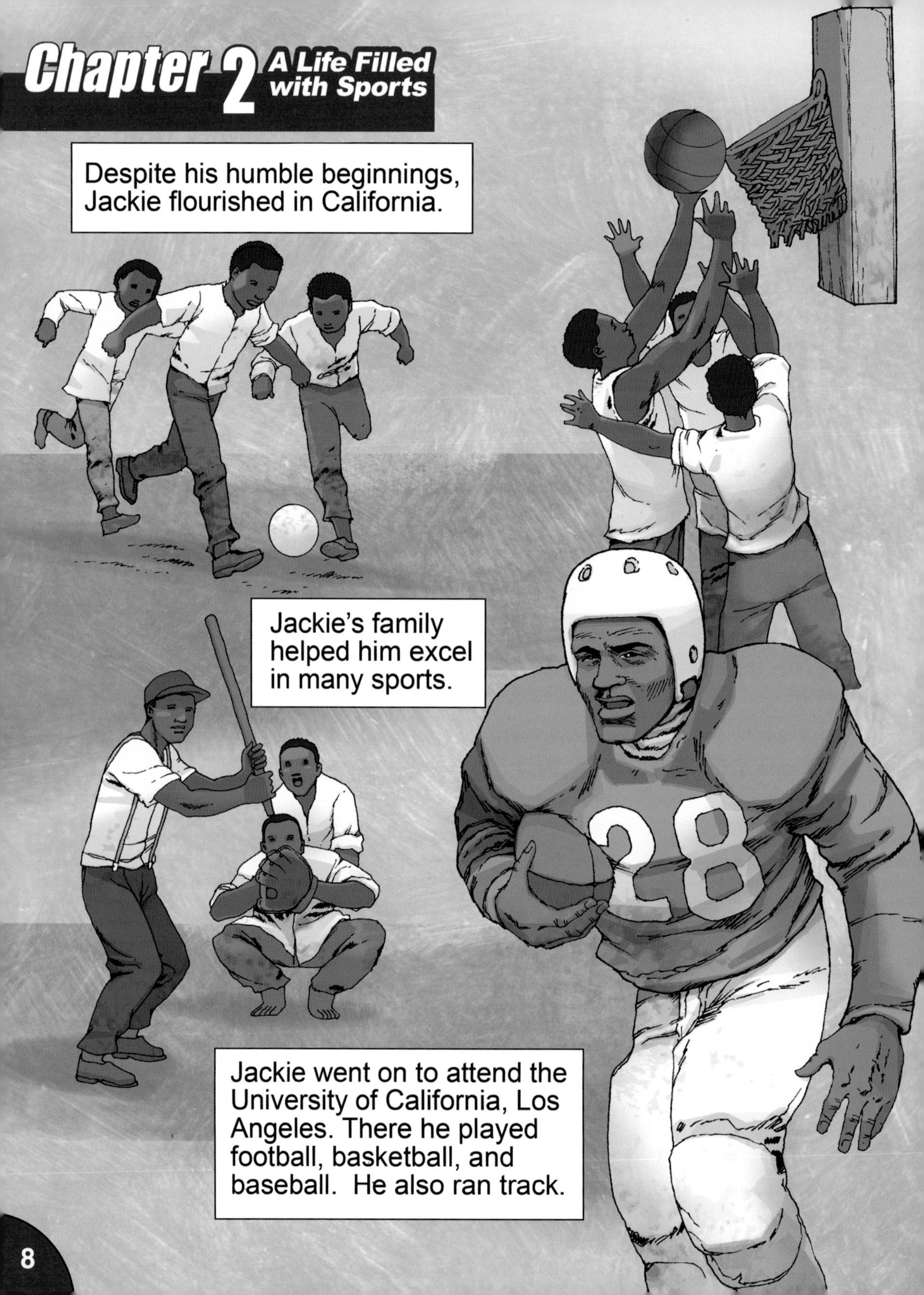
Despite his humble beginnings, Jackie flourished in California.
Jackie's family helped him excel in many sports.
Jackie went on to attend the University of California, Los Angeles. There he played football, basketball, and baseball. He also ran track.
28

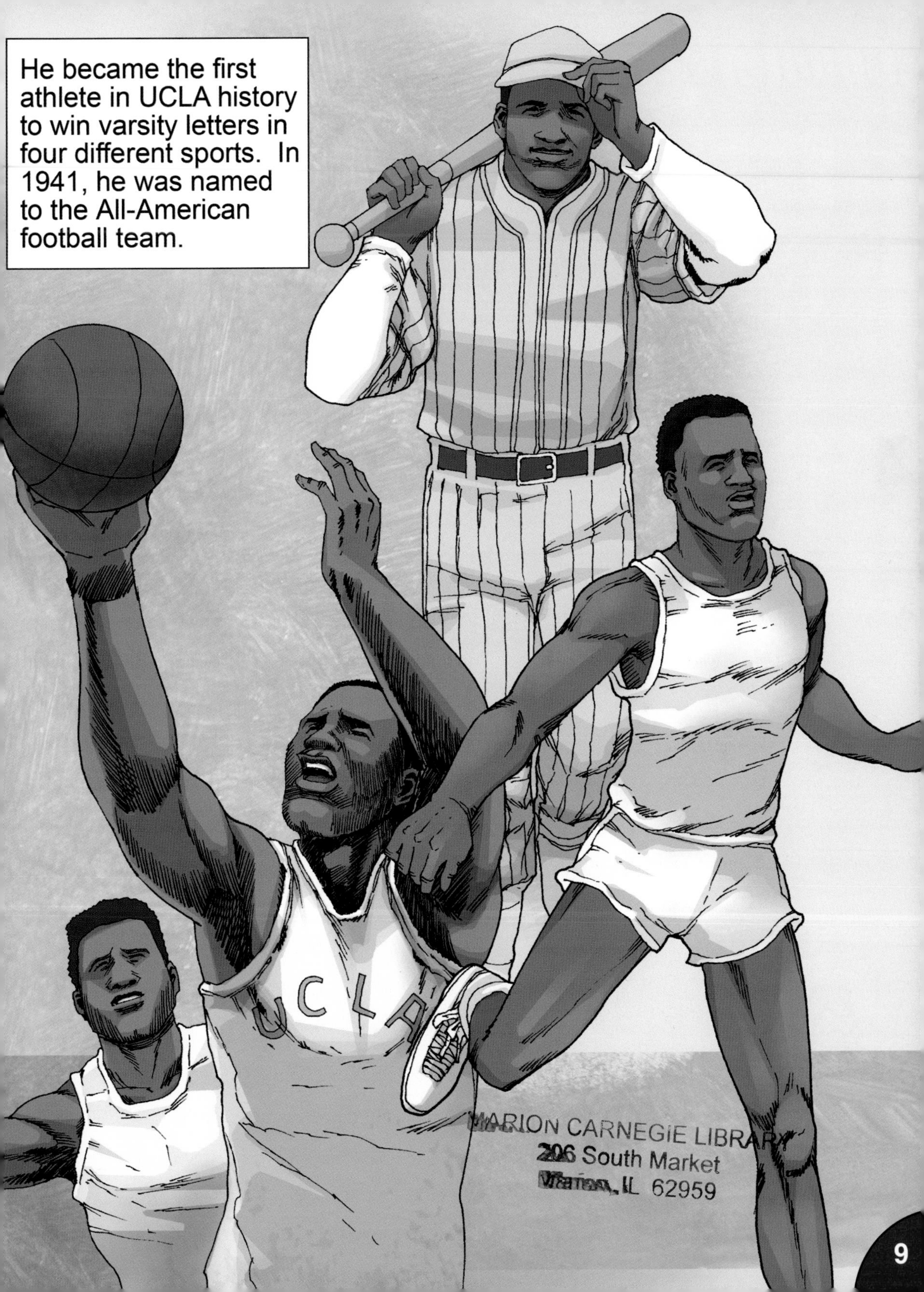
He became the first athlete in UCLA history to win varsity letters in four different sports. In 1941, he was named to the All-American football team.
UCLA

Chapter 3 Military Life

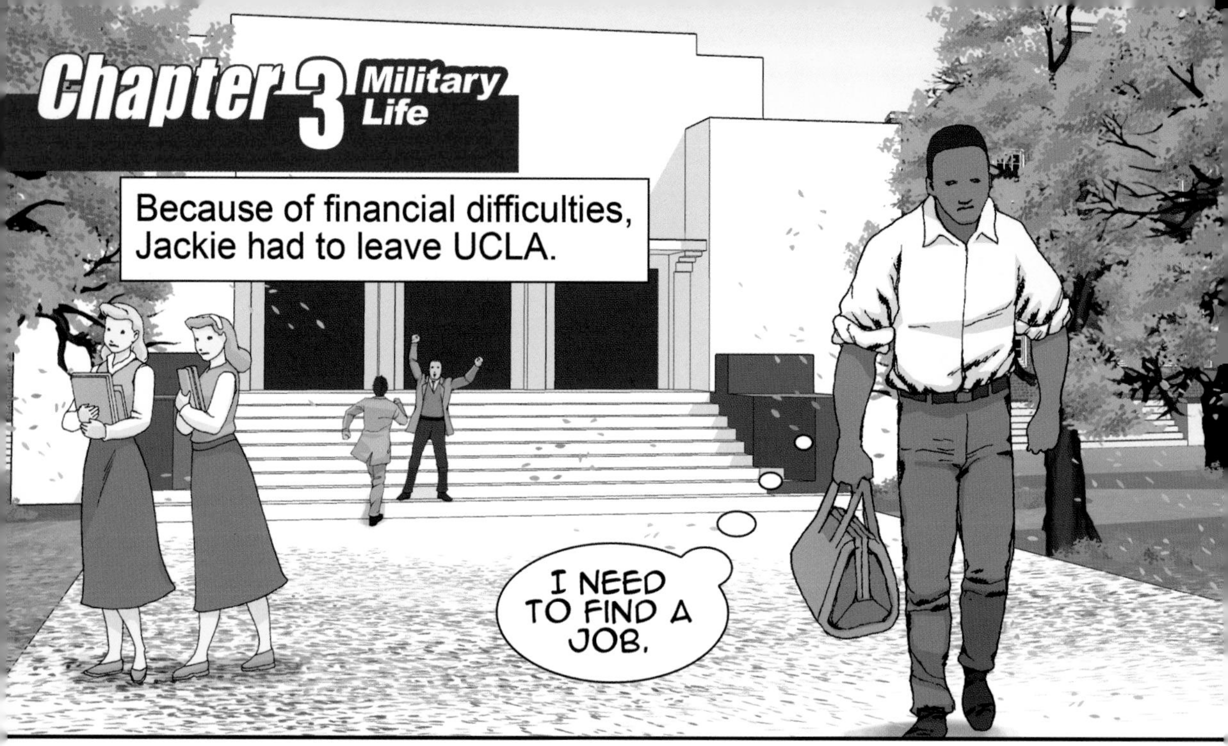
Because of financial difficulties, Jackie had to leave UCLA.
I NEED TO FIND A JOB.

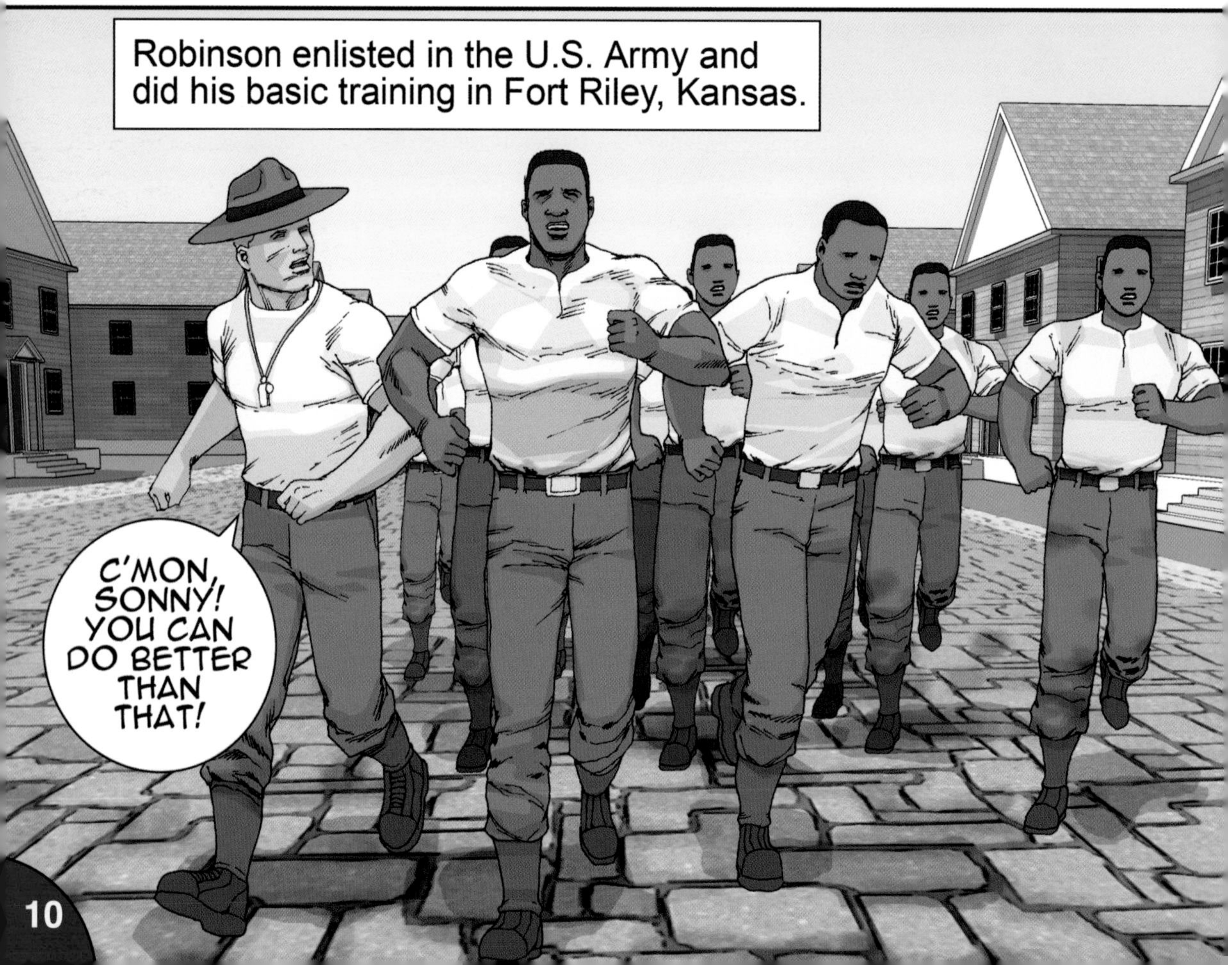
Robinson enlisted in the U.S. Army and did his basic training in Fort Riley, Kansas.
C'MON, SONNY! YOU CAN DO BETTER THAN THAT!

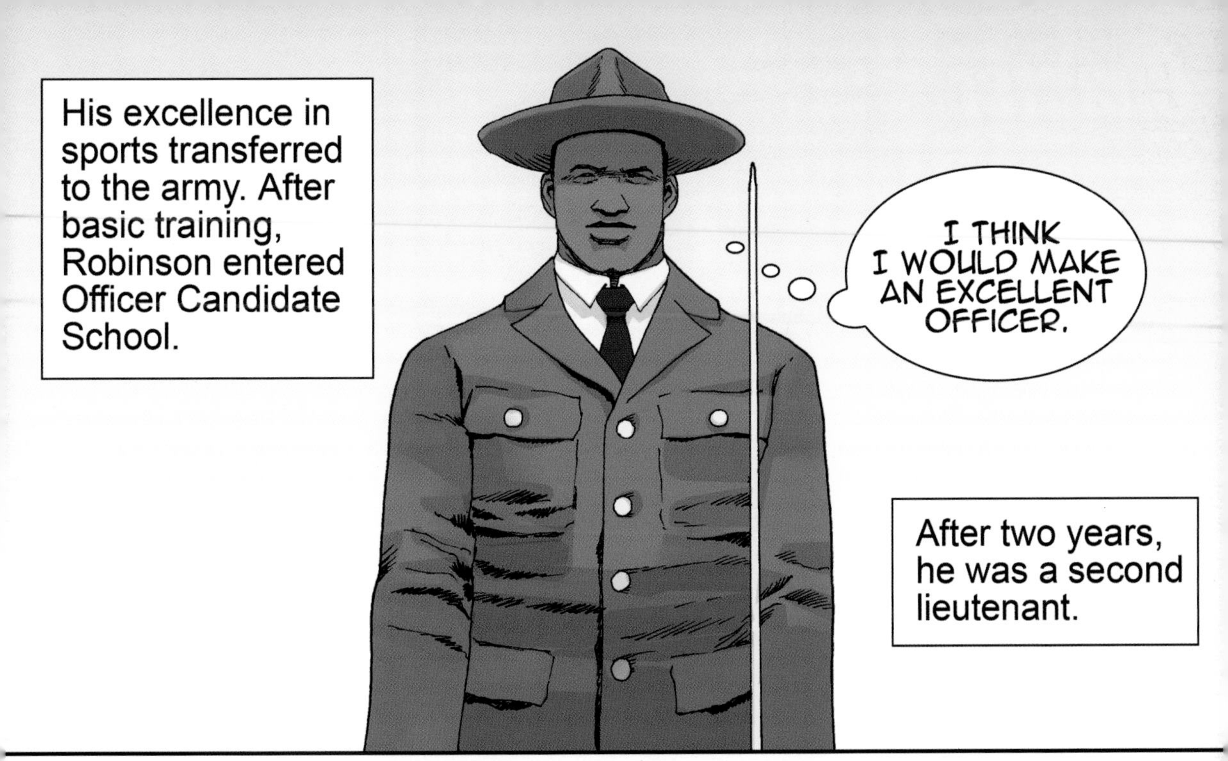
His excellence in sports transferred to the army. After basic training, Robinson entered Officer Candidate School.
I THINK I WOULD MAKE AN EXCELLENT OFFICER.
After two years, he was a second lieutenant.

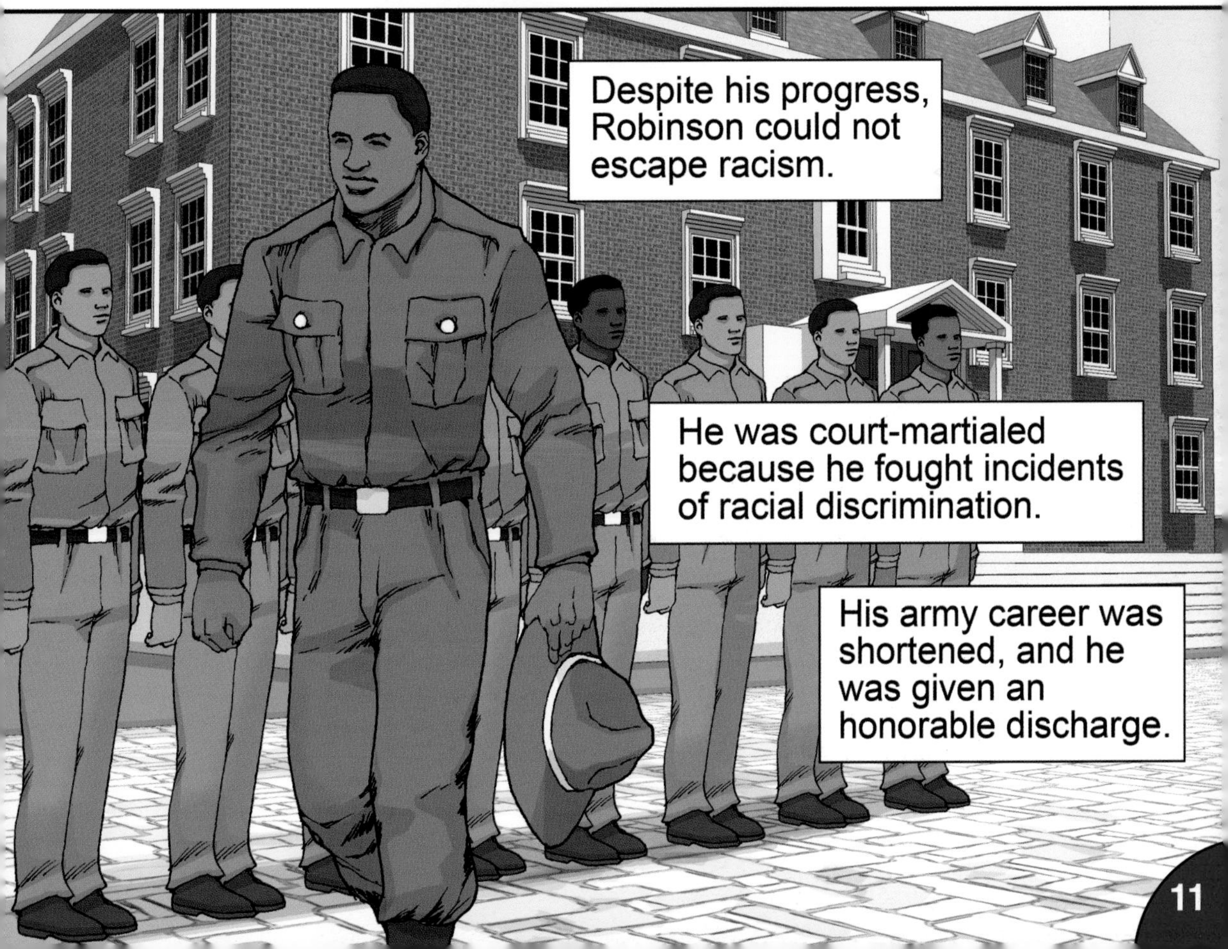
Despite his progress, Robinson could not escape racism.
He was court-martialed because he fought incidents of racial discrimination.
His army career was shortened, and he was given an honorable discharge.

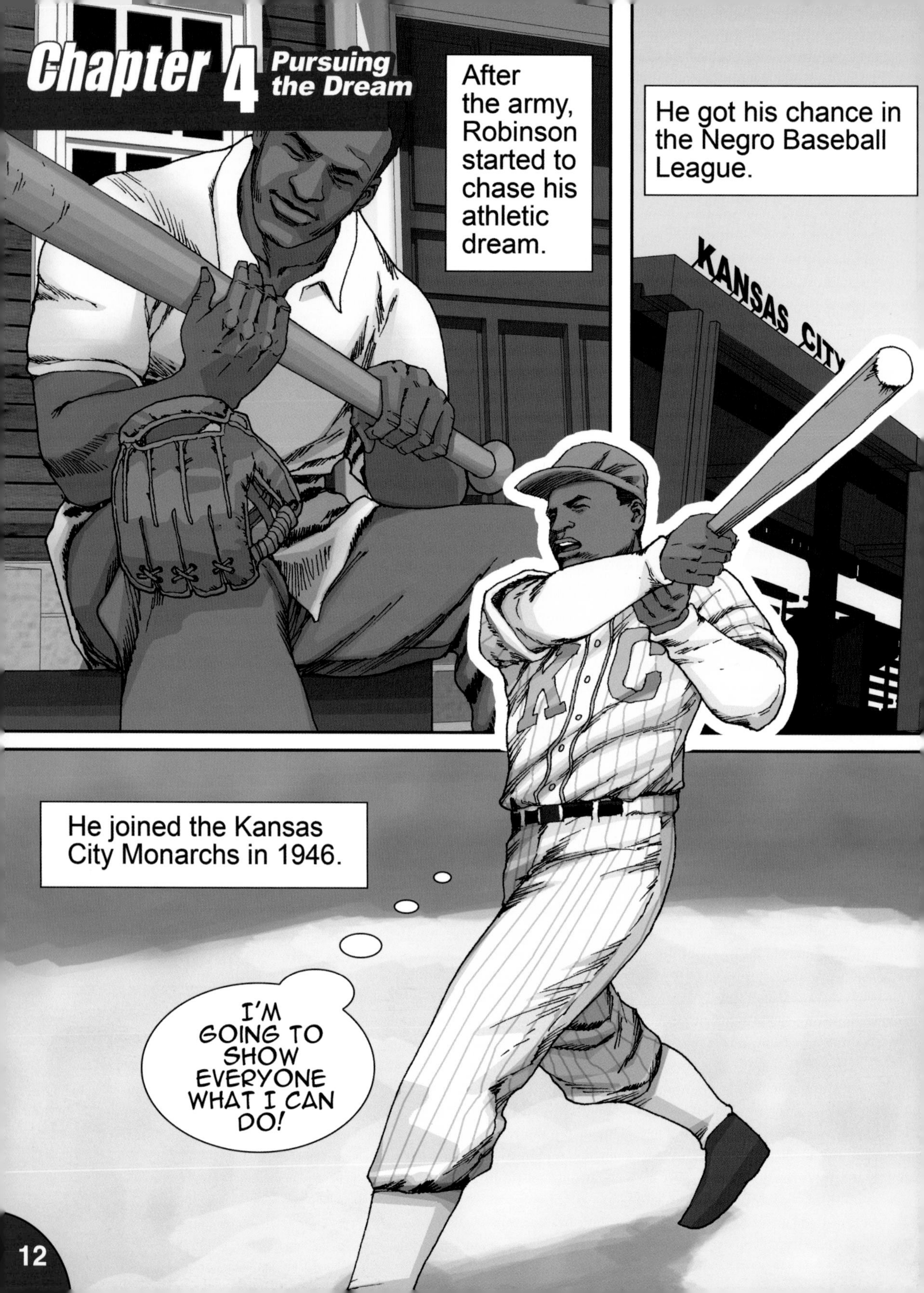

Chapter 4 Pursuing the Dream
After the army, Robinson started to chase his athletic dream.
He got his chance in the Negro Baseball League.
KANSAS CITY
He joined the Kansas City Monarchs in 1946.
I'M GOING TO SHOW EVERYONE WHAT I CAN DO!

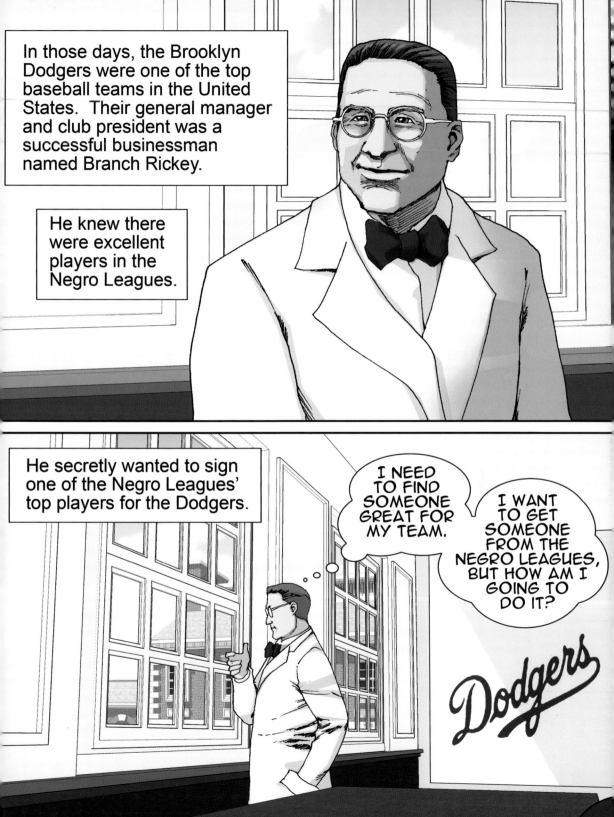

In those days, the Brooklyn Dodgers were one of the top baseball teams in the United States. Their general manager and club president was a successful businessman named Branch Rickey.

He knew there were excellent players in the Negro Leagues.

He secretly wanted to sign one of the Negro Leagues' top players for the Dodgers.

I NEED TO FIND SOMEONE GREAT FOR MY TEAM.

I WANT TO GET SOMEONE FROM THE NEGRO LEAGUES, BUT HOW AM I GOING TO DO IT?

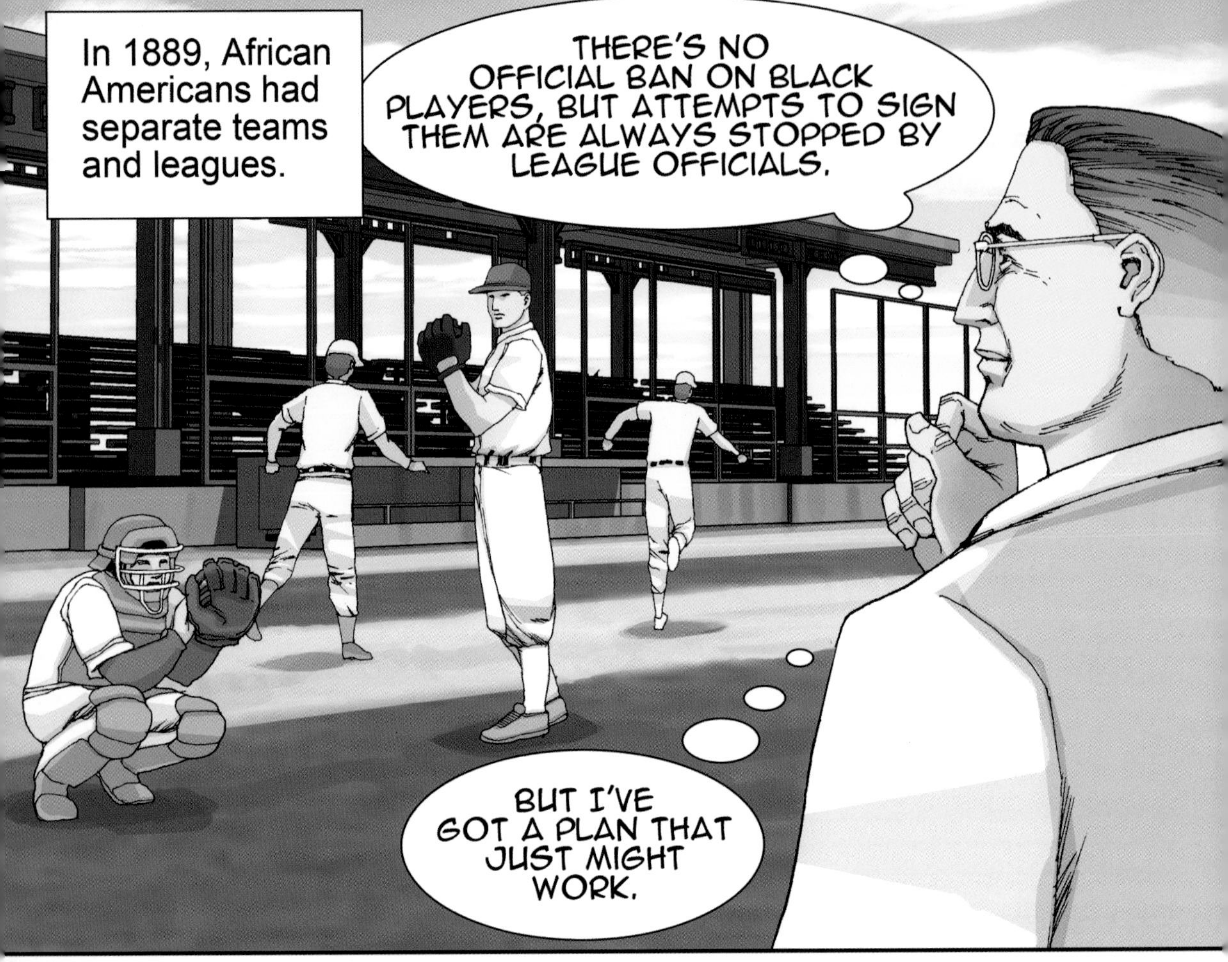
In 1889, African Americans had separate teams and leagues.
THERE'S NO OFFICIAL BAN ON BLACK PLAYERS, BUT ATTEMPTS TO SIGN THEM ARE ALWAYS STOPPED BY LEAGUE OFFICIALS.
BUT I'VE GOT A PLAN THAT JUST MIGHT WORK.

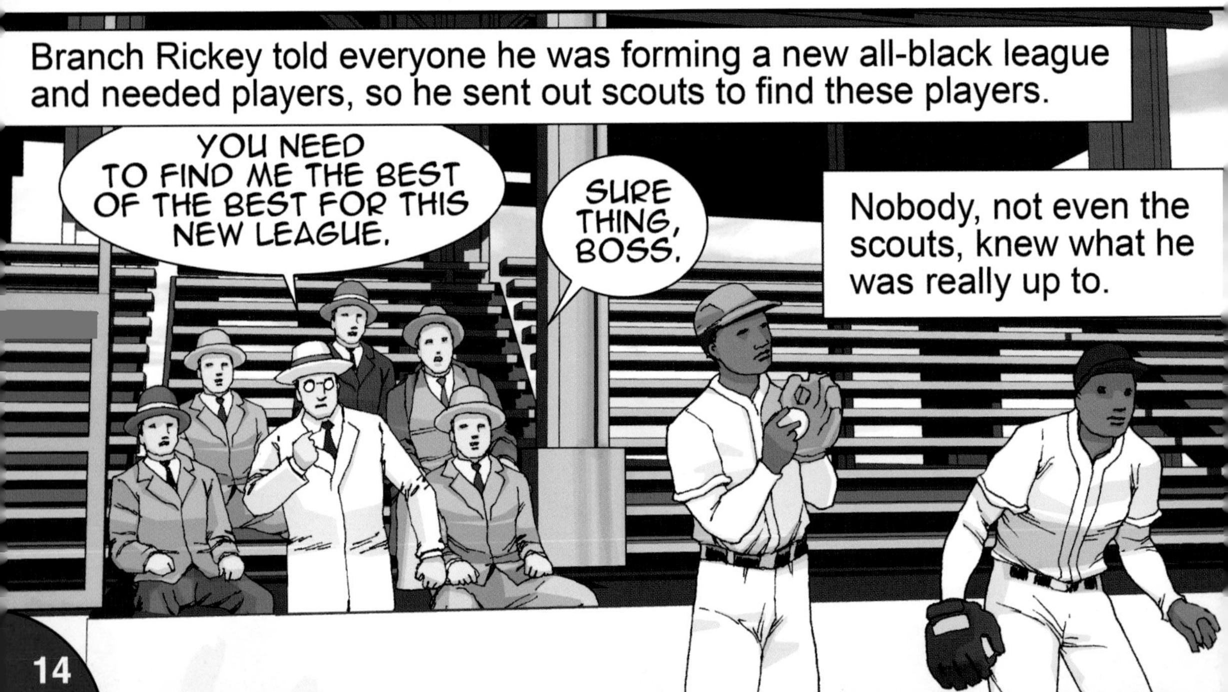
Branch Rickey told everyone he was forming a new all-black league and needed players, so he sent out scouts to find these players.
YOU NEED TO FIND ME THE BEST OF THE BEST FOR THIS NEW LEAGUE.
SURE THING, BOSS.
Nobody, not even the scouts, knew what he was really up to.

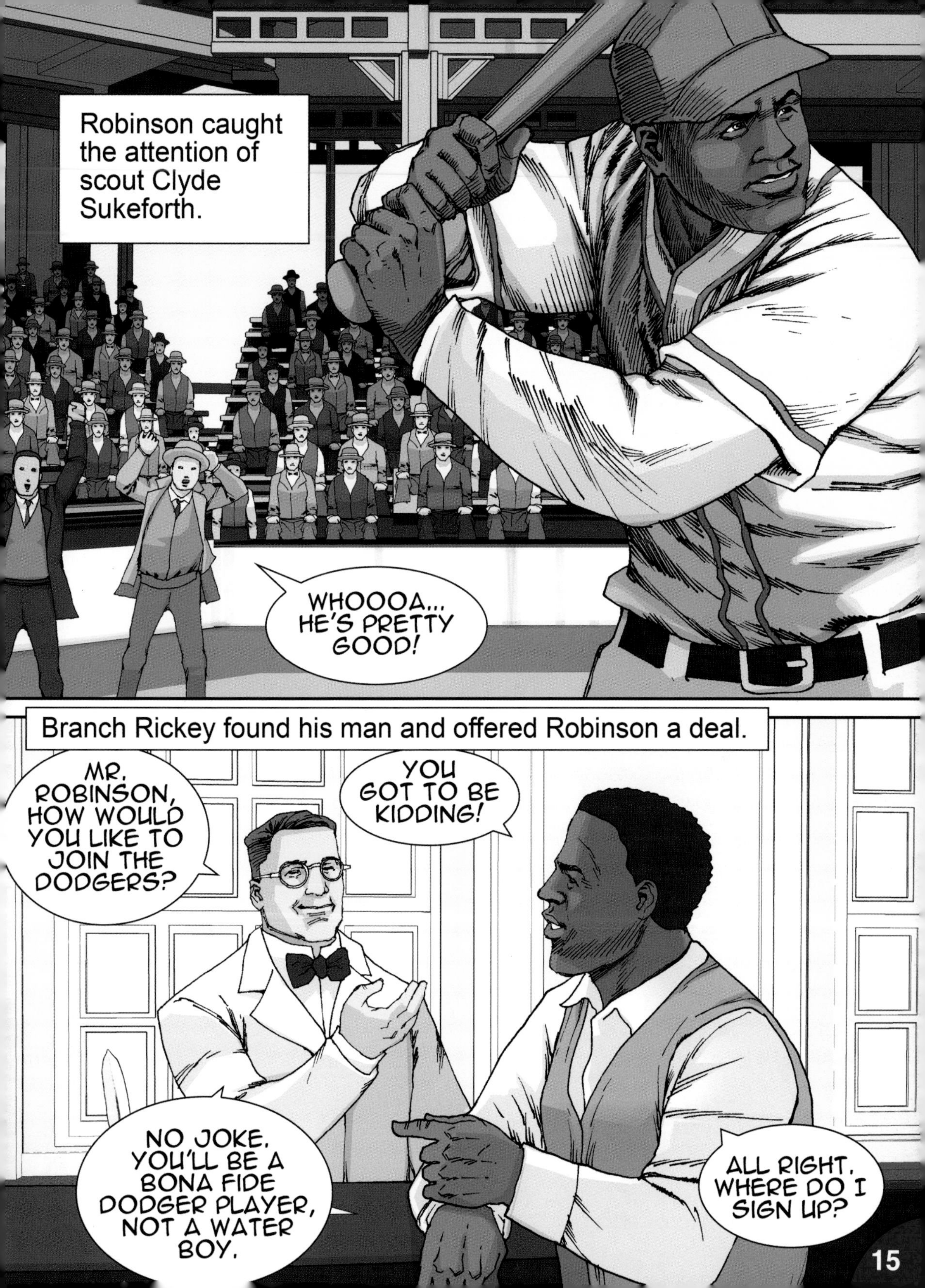
Robinson caught the attention of scout Clyde Sukeforth.
WHOOOA... HE'S PRETTY GOOD!
Branch Rickey found his man and offered Robinson a deal.
MR. ROBINSON, HOW WOULD YOU LIKE TO JOIN THE DODGERS?
YOU GOT TO BE KIDDING!
NO JOKE. YOU'LL BE A BONA FIDE DODGER PLAYER, NOT A WATER BOY.
ALL RIGHT. WHERE DO I SIGN UP?

When Robinson put on the Brooklyn Dodgers uniform, he was the first athlete to integrate professional sports in America. He broke the barrier of racial segregation in the North and South.

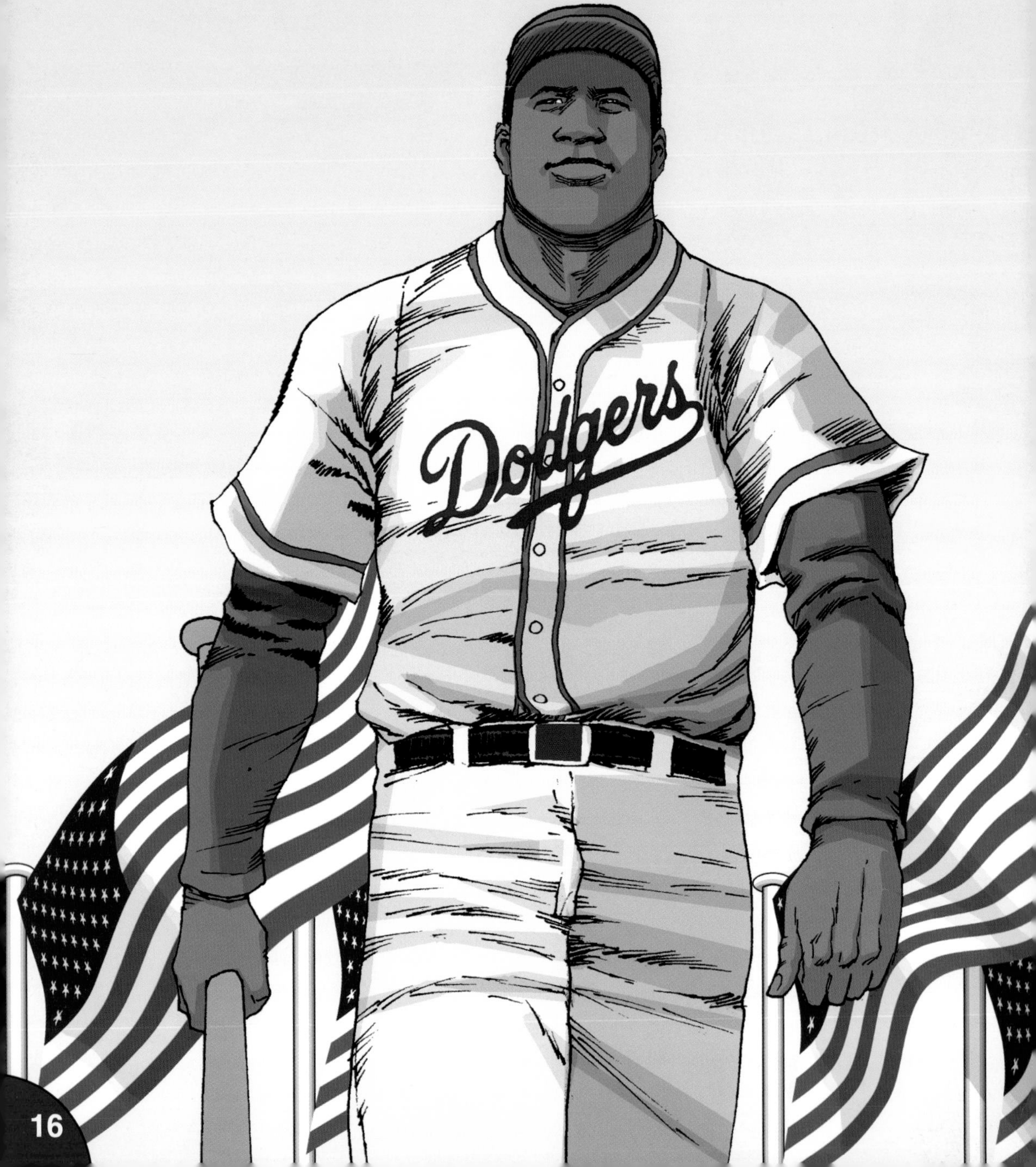
Dodgers

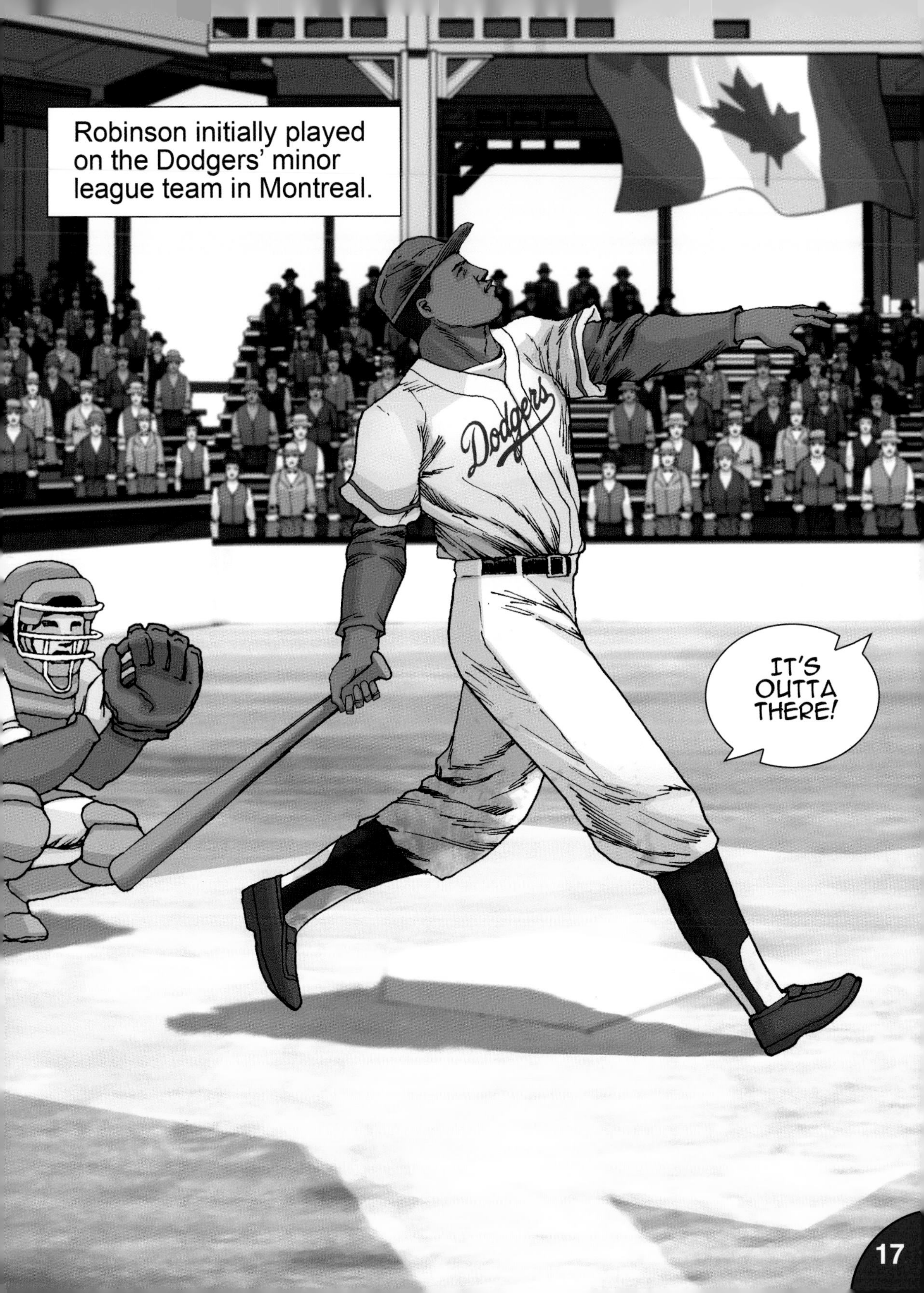

Robinson initially played on the Dodgers' minor league team in Montreal.
Dodgers
IT'S OUTTA THERE!

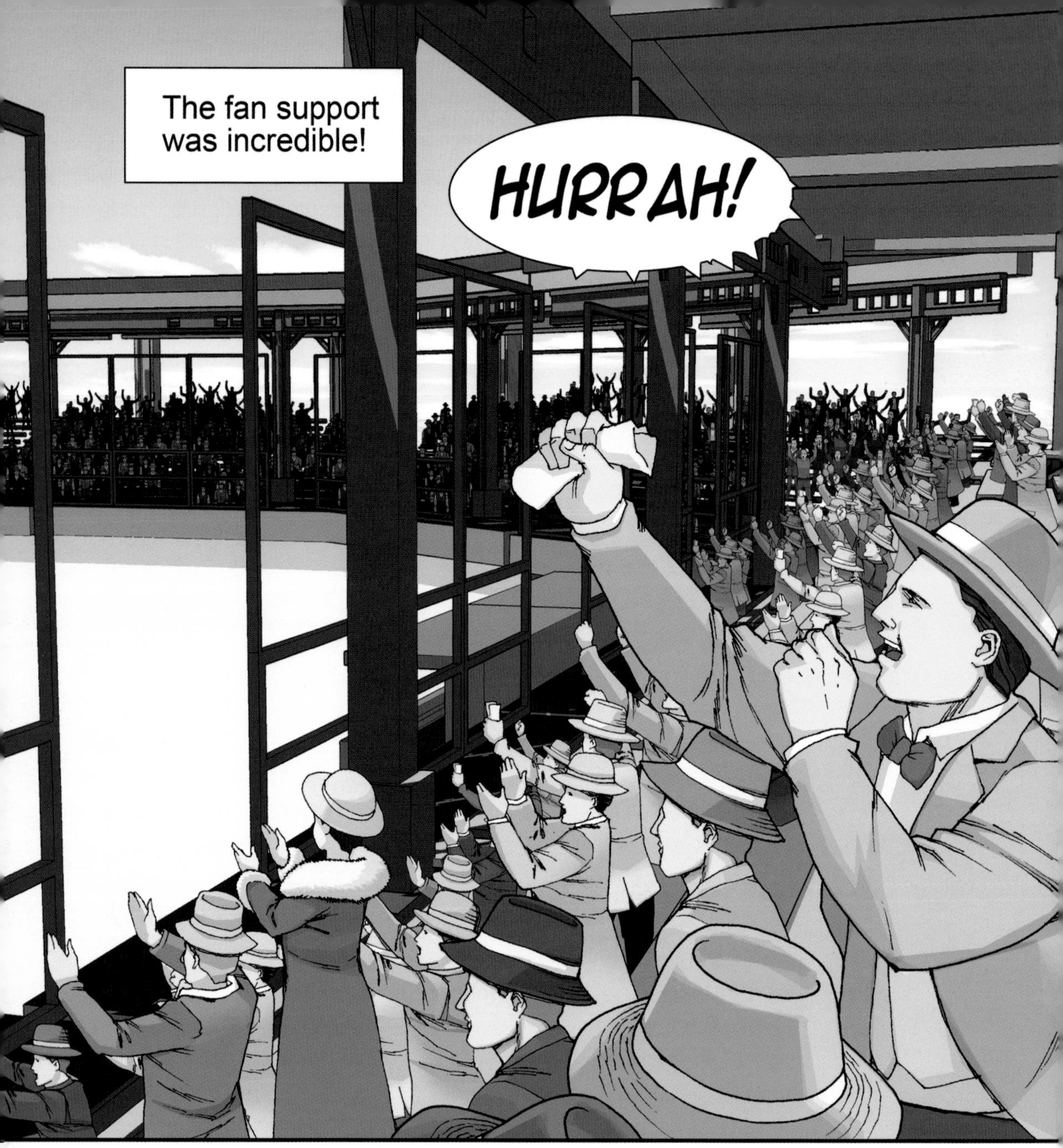
The fan support was incredible!
HURRAH!

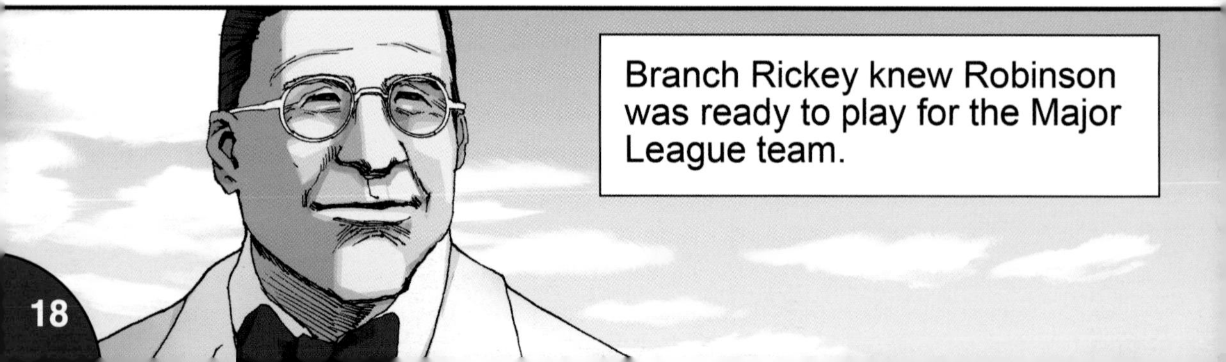
Branch Rickey knew Robinson was ready to play for the Major League team.

Chapter 5 Trials and Tribulations

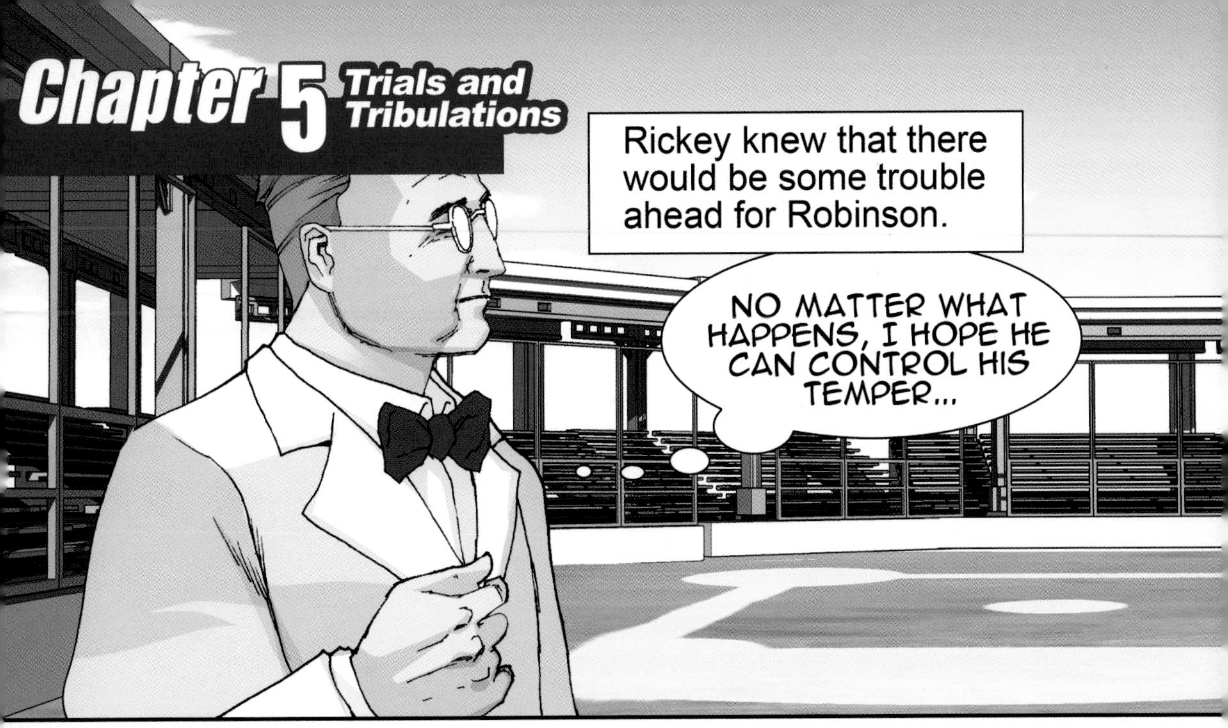
Rickey knew that there would be some trouble ahead for Robinson.
NO MATTER WHAT HAPPENS, I HOPE HE CAN CONTROL HIS TEMPER...

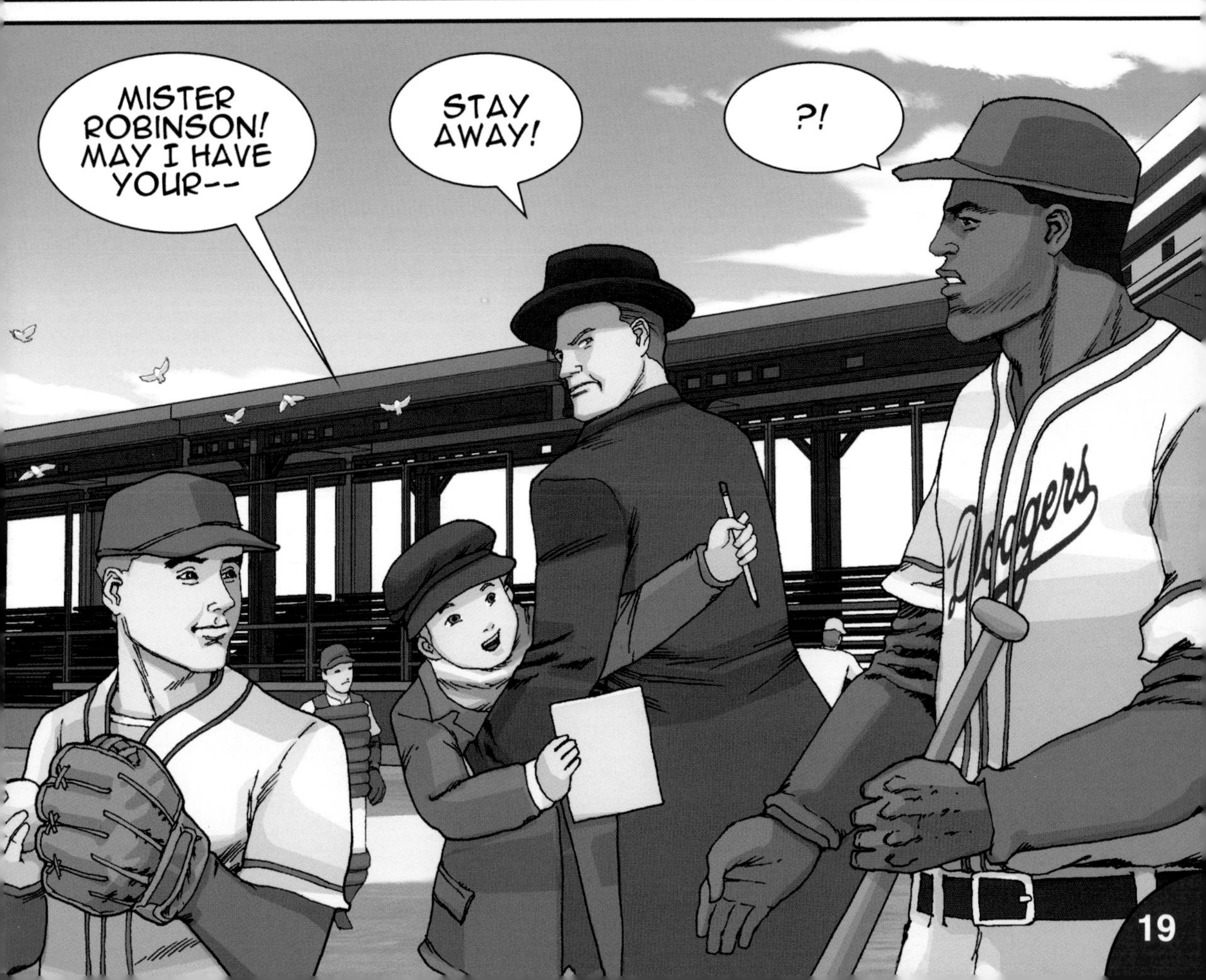
MISTER ROBINSON! MAY I HAVE YOUR--
STAY AWAY!
?!
Dodgers

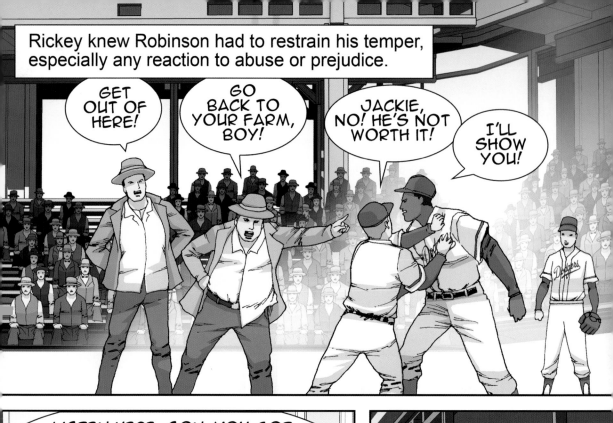

Rickey knew Robinson had to restrain his temper, especially any reaction to abuse or prejudice.

GET OUT OF HERE!

GO BACK TO YOUR FARM, BOY!

JACKIE, NO! HE'S NOT WORTH IT!

I'LL SHOW YOU!

LISTEN HERE, SON. YOU GOT TO IGNORE THOSE INSULTS. LET'S PRACTICE. I'M GONNA SAY SOME BAD THINGS THAT YOU'LL HEAR OUT THERE, BUT YOU'LL IGNORE THEM.

SAY WHAT?

IT'S JUST TO PREPARE YOU. NOW, COME ON. YOU'RE GOING TO GET WORSE OUT THERE.

OK, I CAN TAKE IT!

Robinson's first game with the Dodgers was on April 15, 1947. He played first base and batted 0 for 3.

ARE YOU PLANNING TO TOP YOUR GAME IN MONTREAL, MR. ROBINSON?

YOU AIN'T SEEN NOTHING YET.

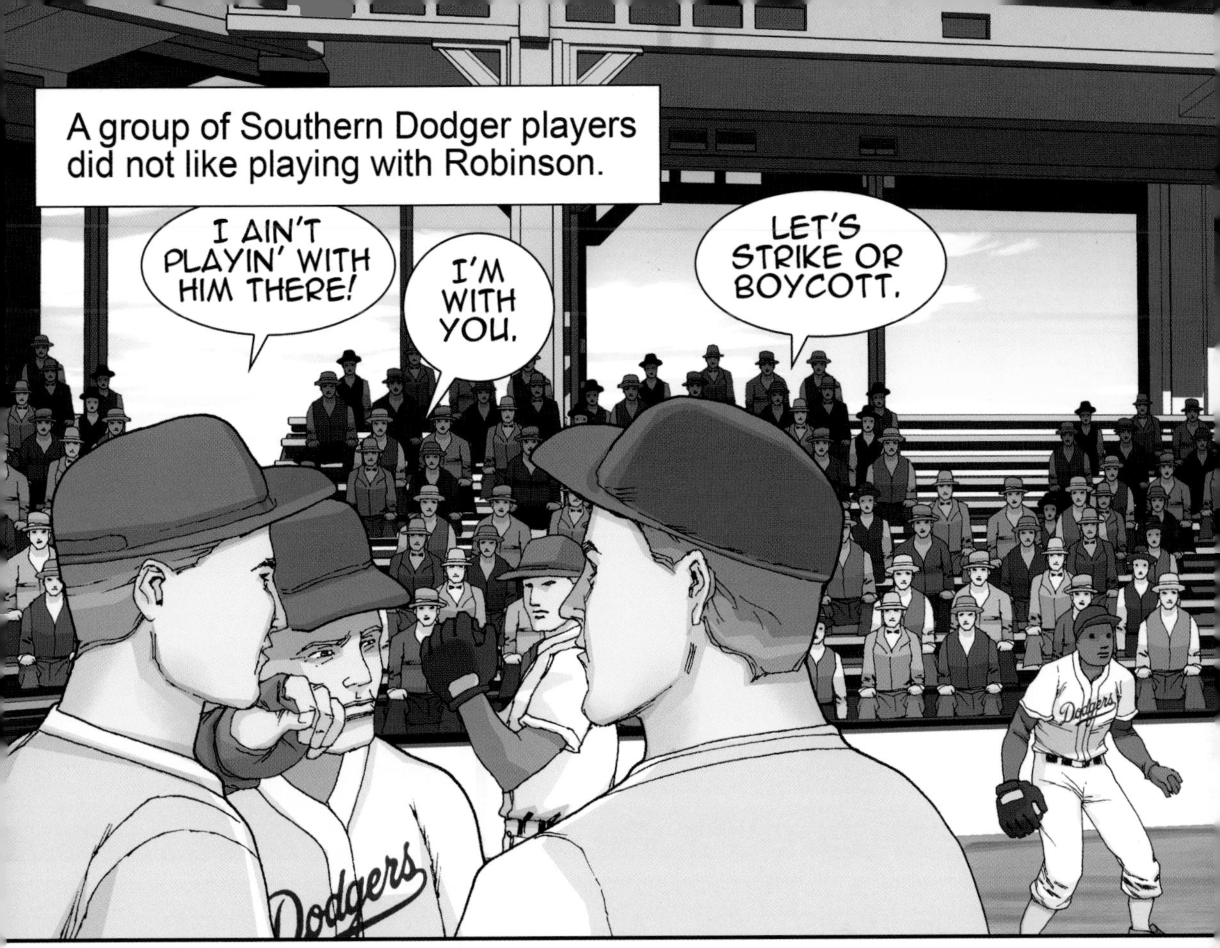
A group of Southern Dodger players did not like playing with Robinson.
I AIN'T PLAYIN' WITH HIM THERE!
I'M WITH YOU.
LET'S STRIKE OR BOYCOTT.

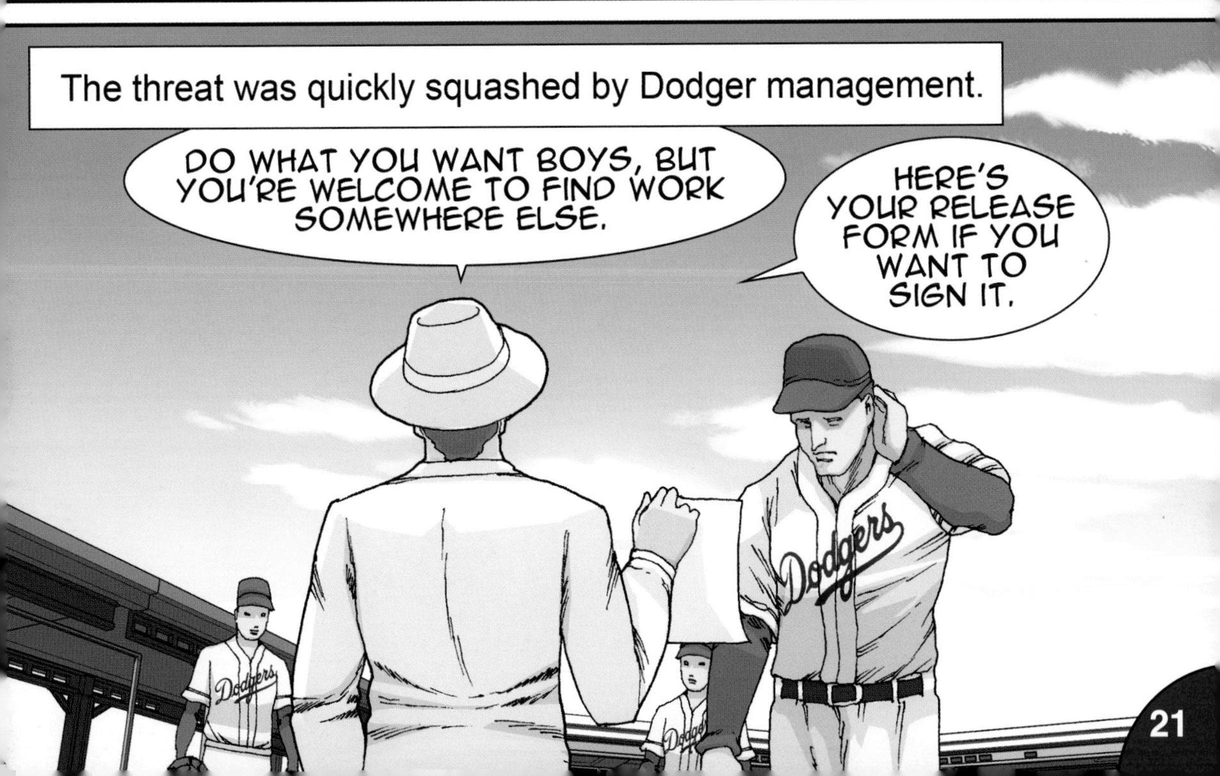
The threat was quickly squashed by Dodger management.
DO WHAT YOU WANT BOYS, BUT YOU'RE WELCOME TO FIND WORK SOMEWHERE ELSE.
HERE'S YOUR RELEASE FORM IF YOU WANT TO SIGN IT.

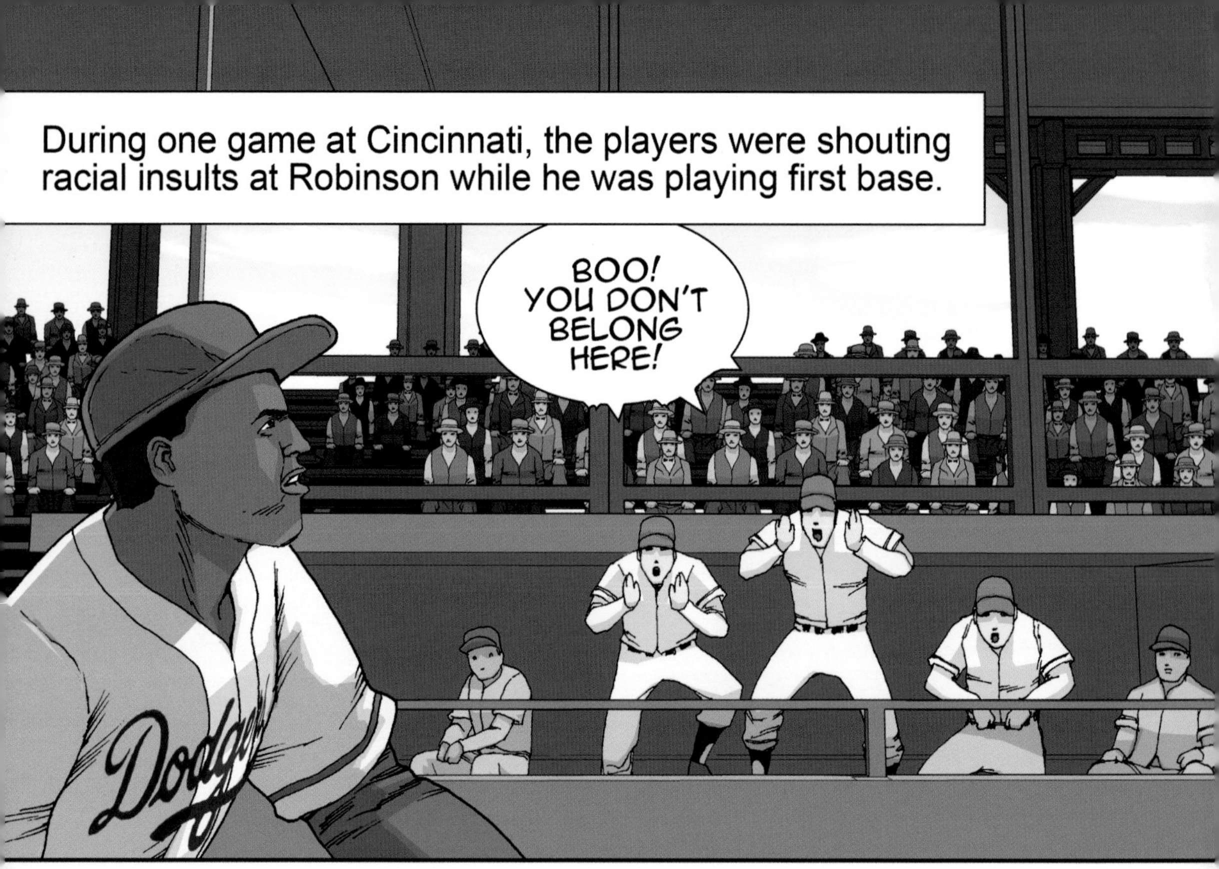
During one game at Cincinnati, the players were shouting racial insults at Robinson while he was playing first base.
BOO! YOU DON'T BELONG HERE!

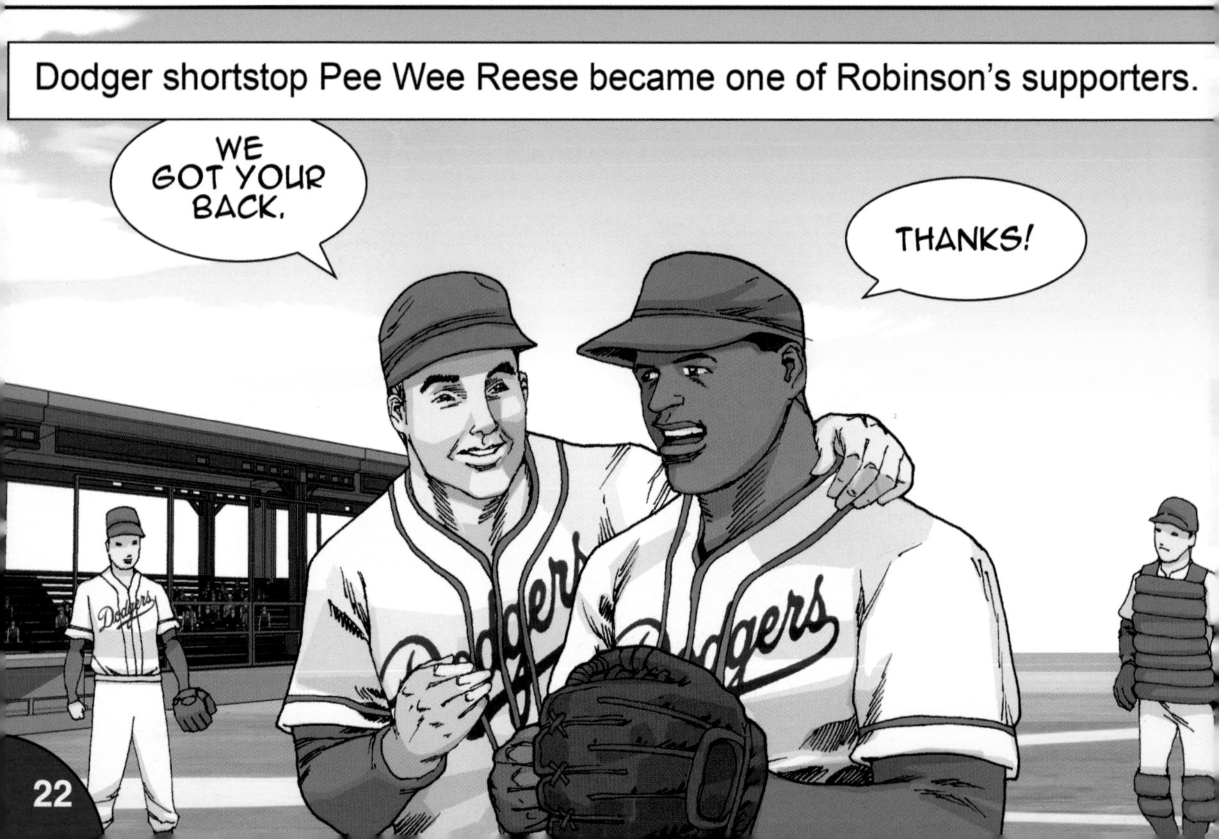
Dodger shortstop Pee Wee Reese became one of Robinson's supporters.
WE GOT YOUR BACK.
THANKS!

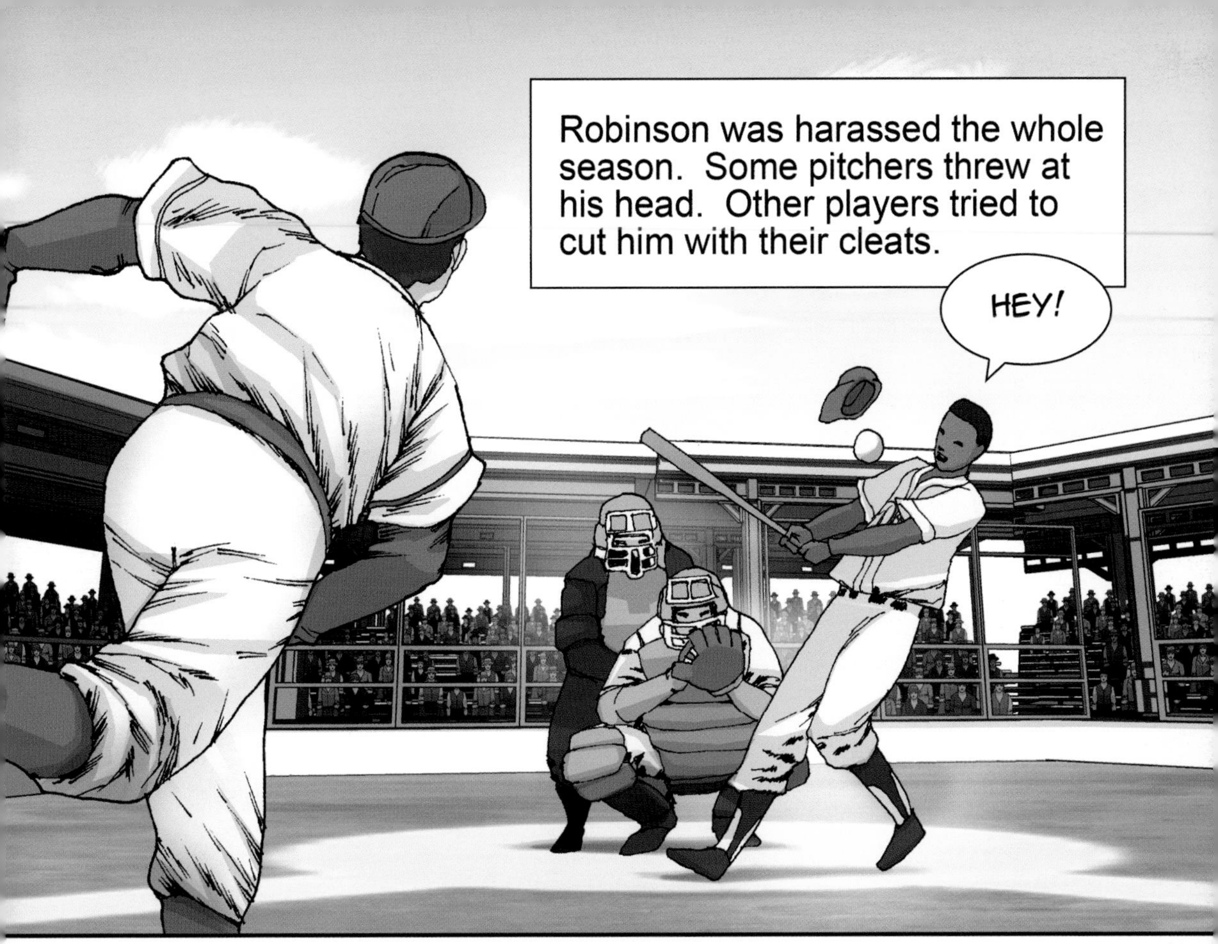
Robinson was harassed the whole season. Some pitchers threw at his head. Other players tried to cut him with their cleats.
HEY!

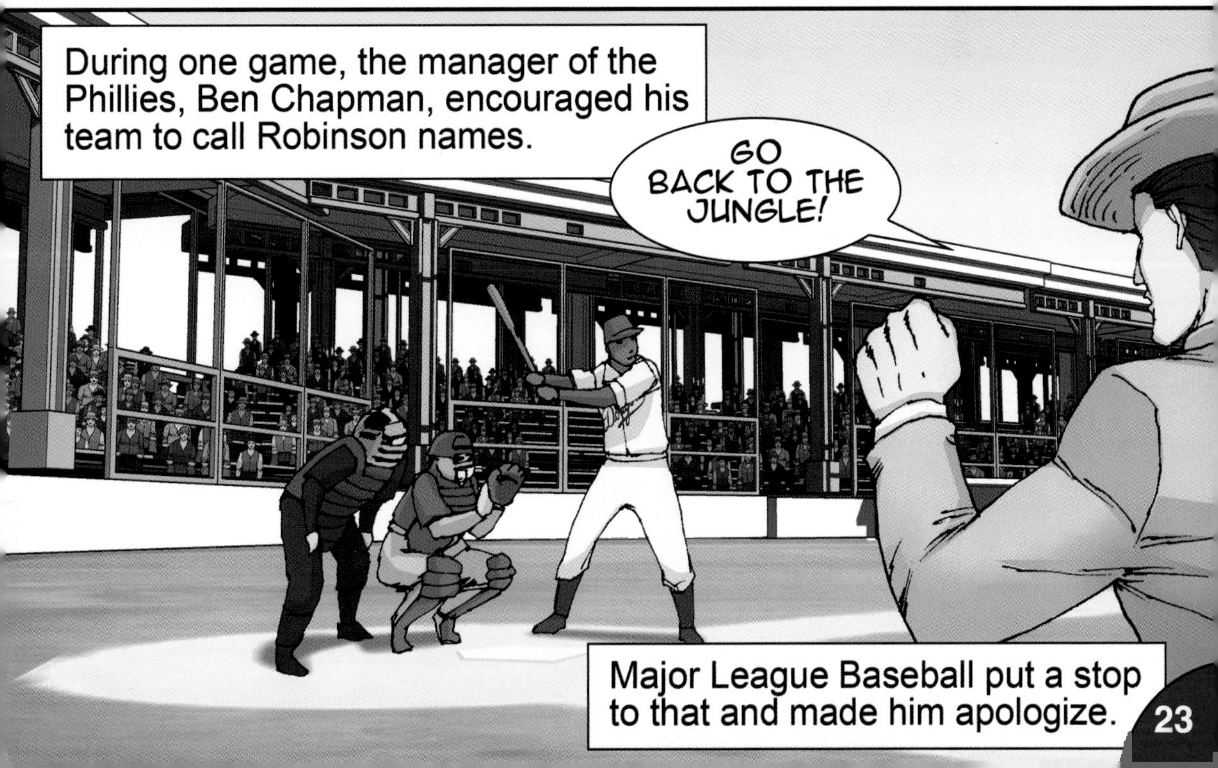
During one game, the manager of the Phillies, Ben Chapman, encouraged his team to call Robinson names.
GO BACK TO THE JUNGLE!
Major League Baseball put a stop to that and made him apologize.

Chapter 6 Jackie Wins Over the Fans!

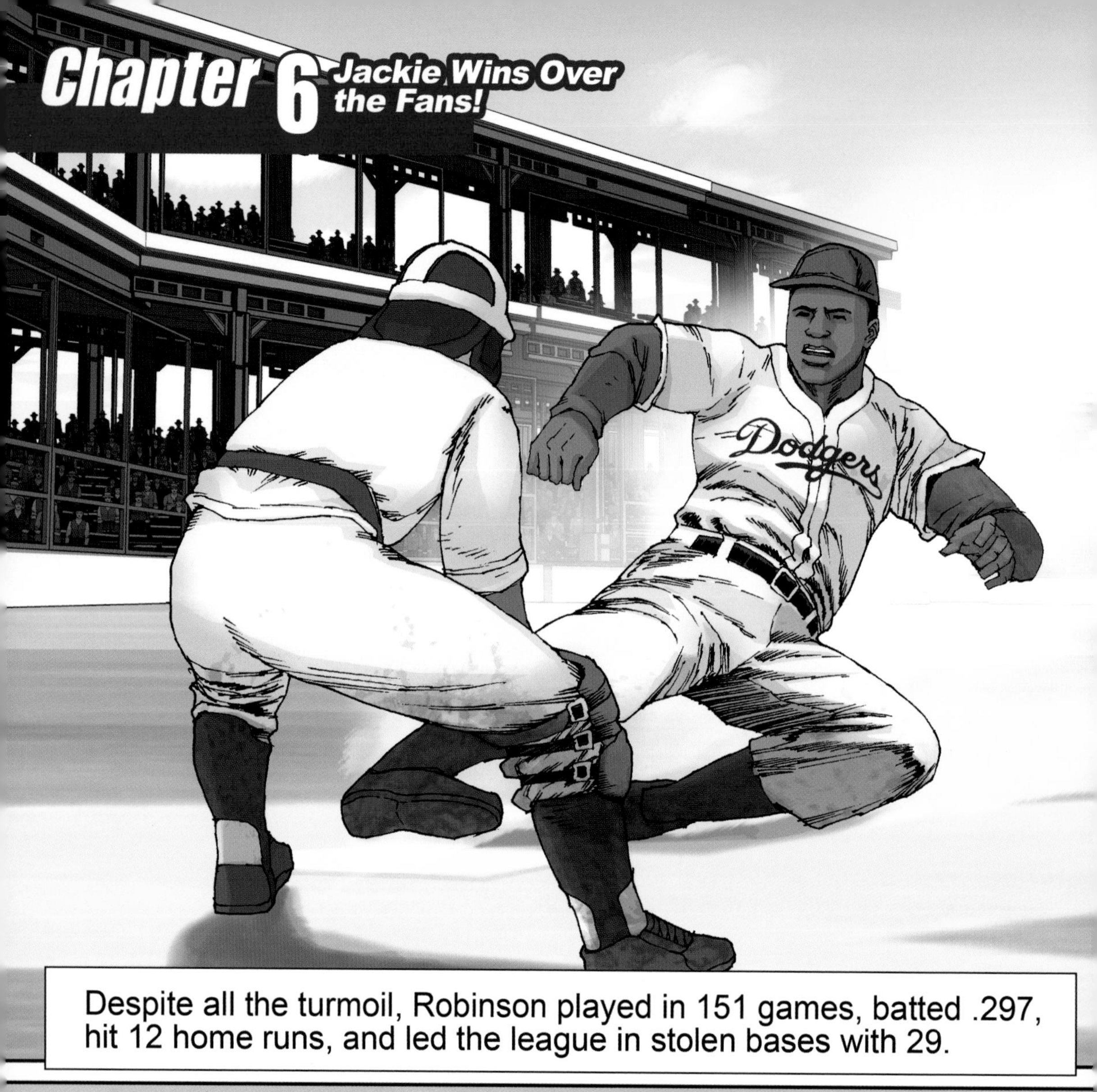
Dodgers
Despite all the turmoil, Robinson played in 151 games, batted .297, hit 12 home runs, and led the league in stolen bases with 29.

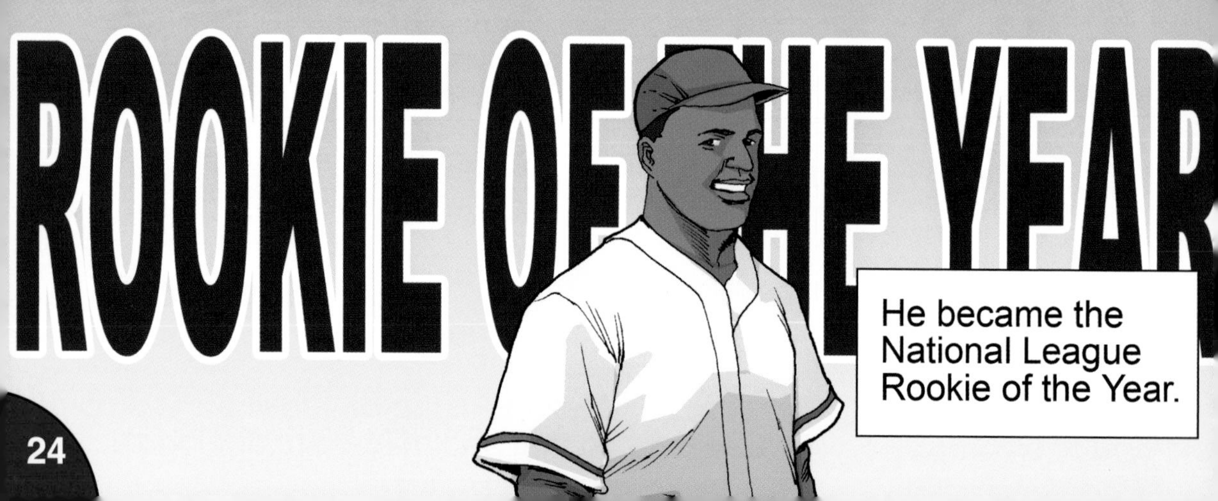
He became the National League Rookie of the Year.

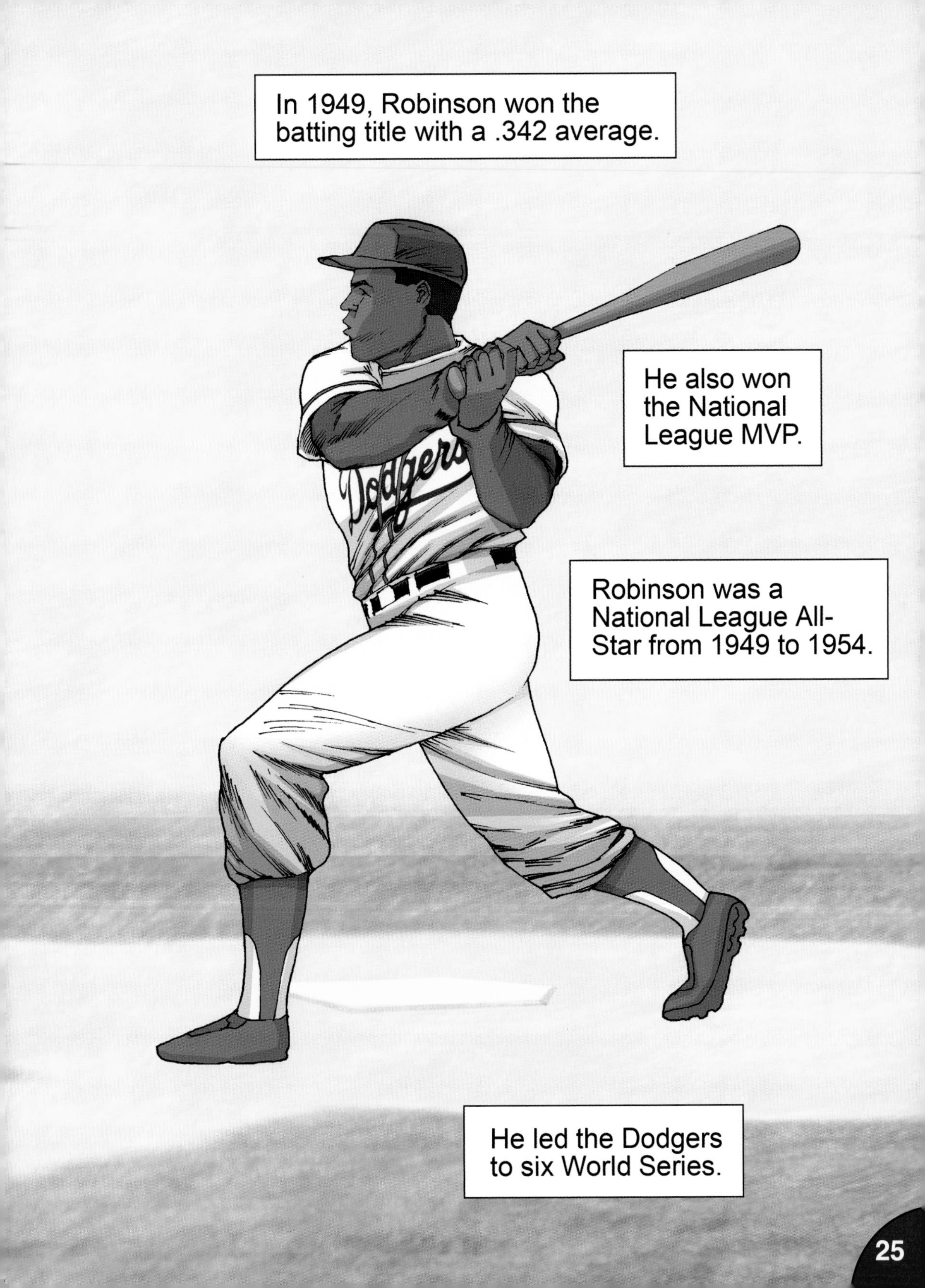
In 1949, Robinson won the batting title with a .342 average.
He also won the National League MVP.
Dodgers
Robinson was a National League All-Star from 1949 to 1954.
He led the Dodgers to six World Series.

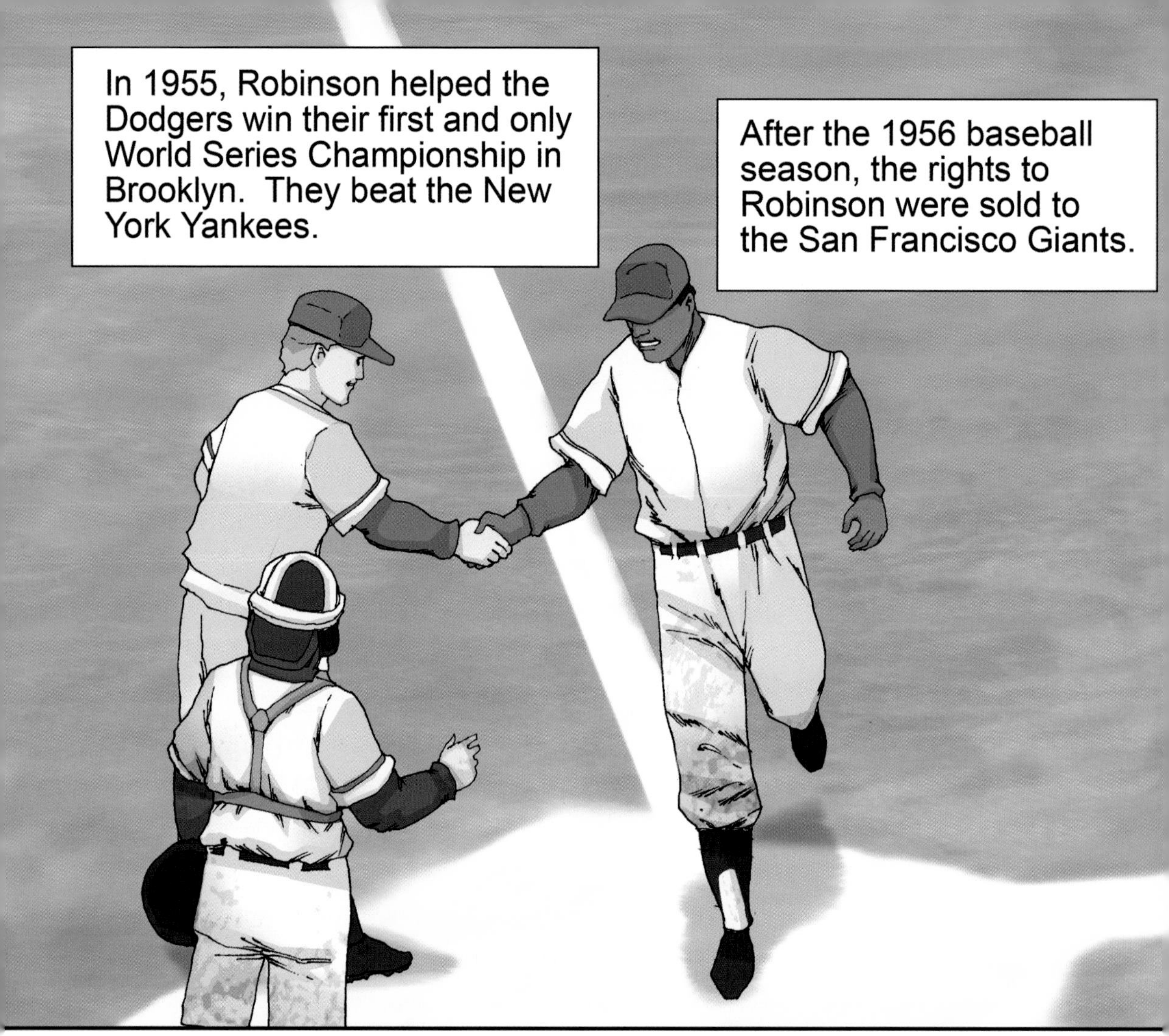
In 1955, Robinson helped the Dodgers win their first and only World Series Championship in Brooklyn. They beat the New York Yankees.
After the 1956 baseball season, the rights to Robinson were sold to the San Francisco Giants.

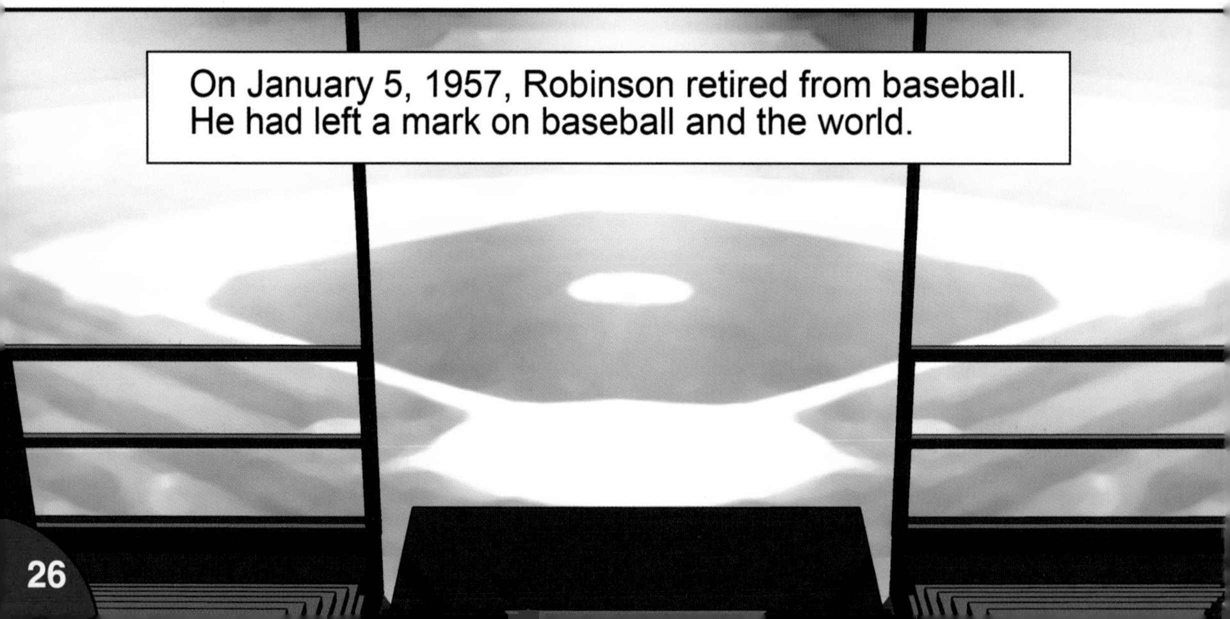
On January 5, 1957, Robinson retired from baseball. He had left a mark on baseball and the world.

In 1962, Robinson was inducted to the Baseball Hall of Fame. He was the first African American to be honored. On June 4, 1972, his Dodger uniform number (42) was retired.

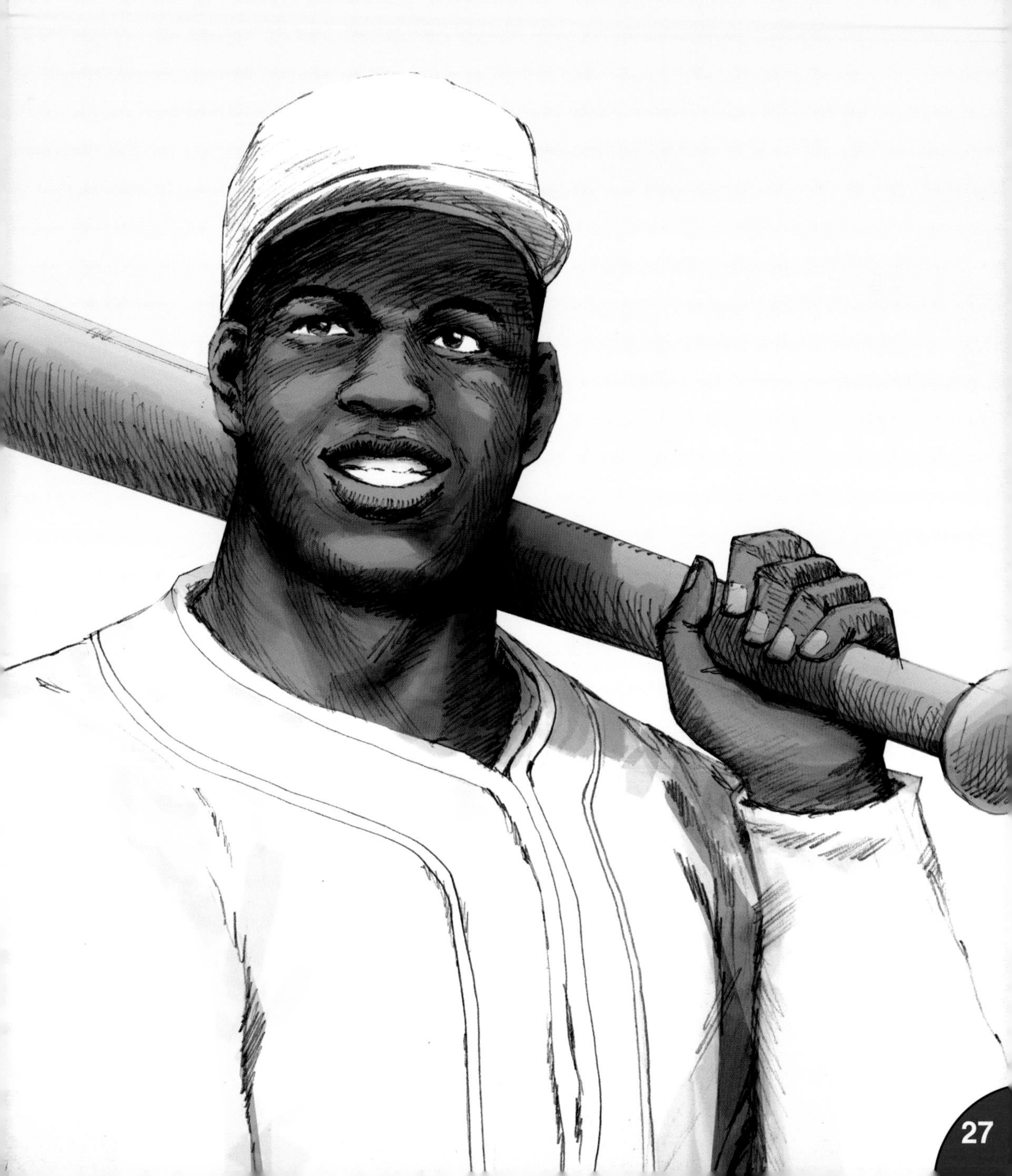

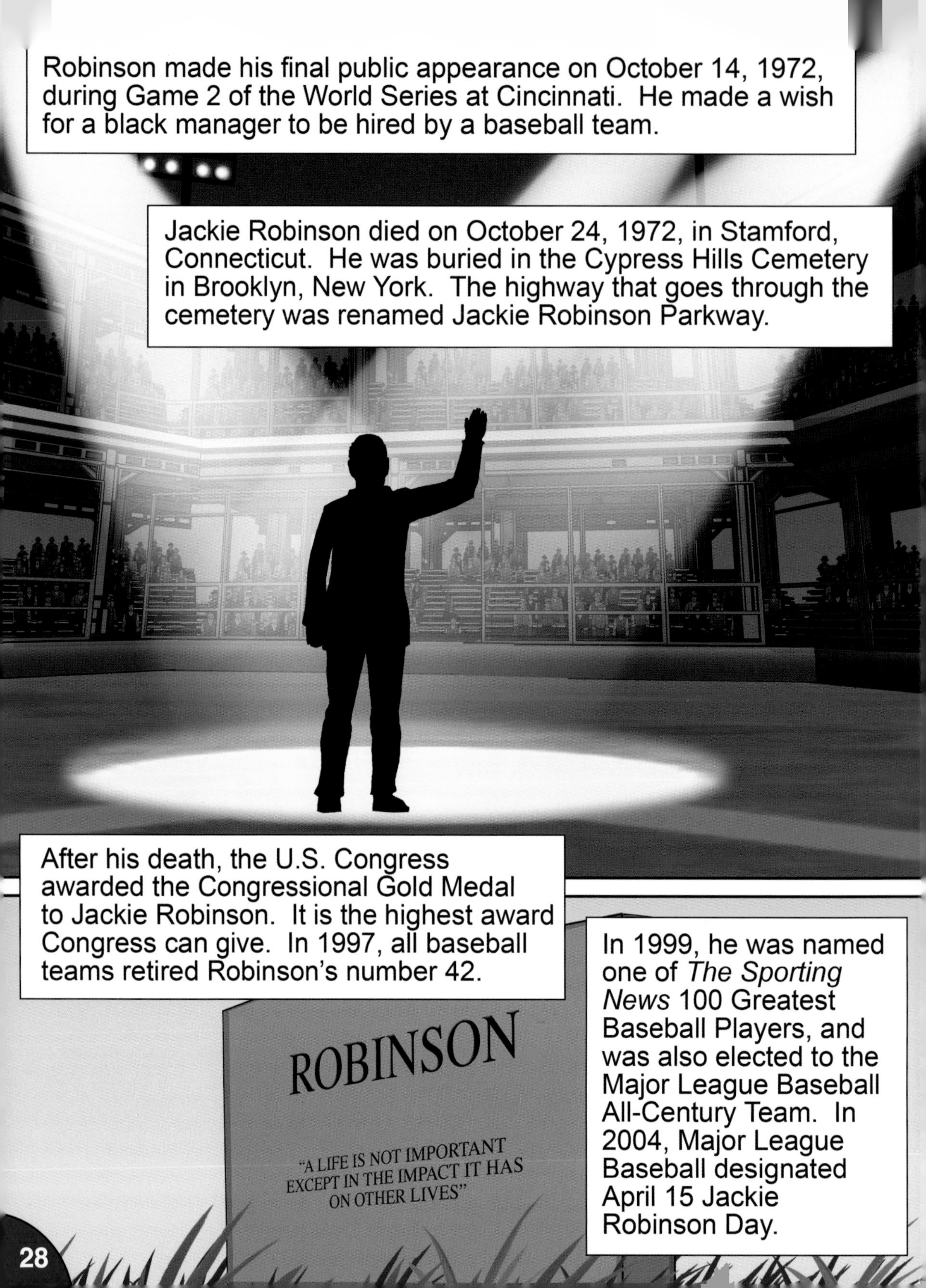
Robinson made his final public appearance on October 14, 1972, during Game 2 of the World Series at Cincinnati. He made a wish for a black manager to be hired by a baseball team.
Jackie Robinson died on October 24, 1972, in Stamford, Connecticut. He was buried in the Cypress Hills Cemetery in Brooklyn, New York. The highway that goes through the cemetery was renamed Jackie Robinson Parkway.
After his death, the U.S. Congress awarded the Congressional Gold Medal to Jackie Robinson. It is the highest award Congress can give. In 1997, all baseball teams retired Robinson's number 42.
In 1999, he was named one of *The Sporting News* 100 Greatest Baseball Players, and was also elected to the Major League Baseball All-Century Team. In 2004, Major League Baseball designated April 15 Jackie Robinson Day.
ROBINSON
"A LIFE IS NOT IMPORTANT EXCEPT IN THE IMPACT IT HAS ON OTHER LIVES"

Major League Team: **Brooklyn Dodgers (1947-1957)**
Jersey Number: **42**
Position: **Second Base**

Games Played:	**1,382**
Career At Bats:	**4,877**
Career Hits:	**1,518**
Career Home Runs:	**137**
Career RBIs:	**734**
Career Batting Average:	**.311**

Led Team to Win League Championship: **6 times**
Led Team to Win World Series Championship: **1 time**
Awards: **Rookie of the Year in 1947**
       National League MVP in 1949
       All-Star every year from 1949 to 1954

Further Reading

Elish, Dan. *Jackie Robinson*. New York: Scholastic Library Publishing, 2005.

Hanft, Joshua E. *Jackie Robinson*. Heroes of America. Edina: ABDO Publishing Company, 2005.

Patrick, Denise Lewis. *Jackie Robinson: Strong Inside and Out*. New York: HarperCollins Publishers, 2005.

Wheeler, Jill C. *Jackie Robinson*. Breaking Barriers. Edina: ABDO Publishing Company, 2003.

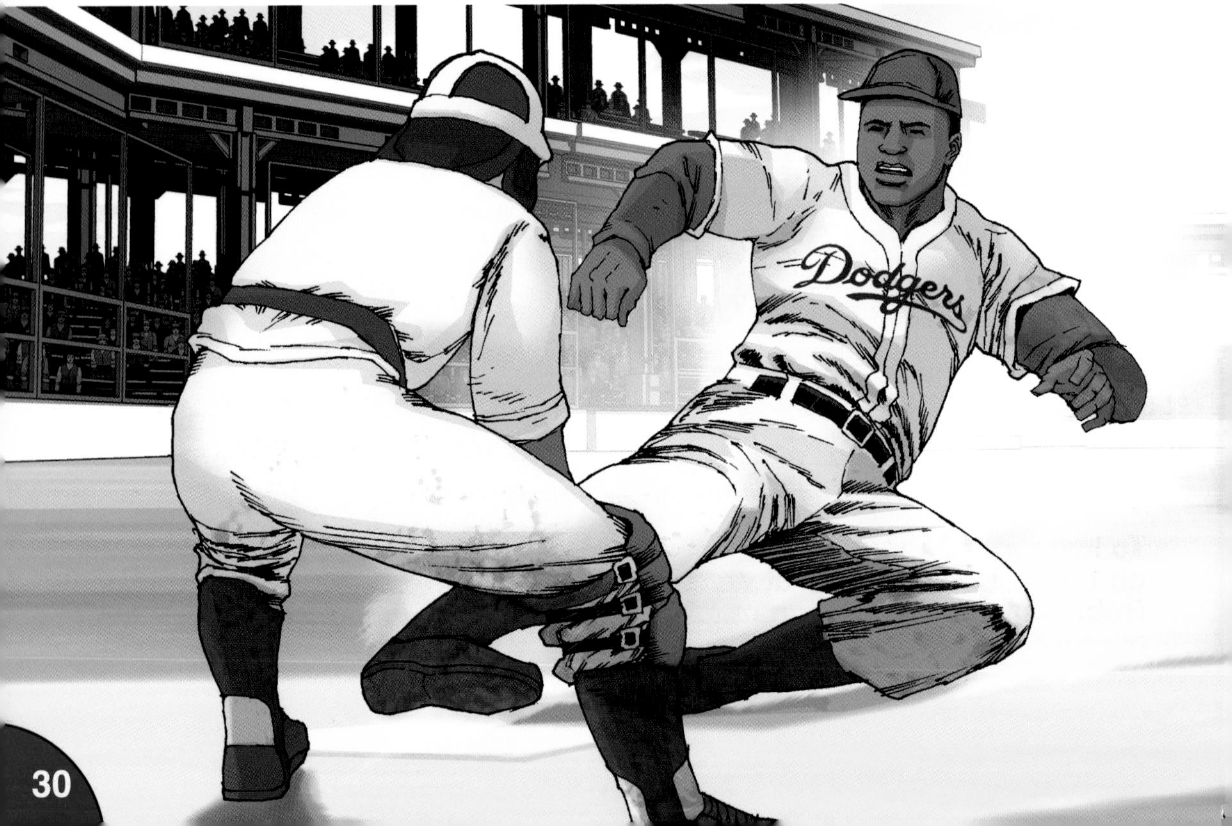
Dodgers

Glossary

basic training - the training period U.S. military recruits complete before they enter battle.

court-martial - a military court that tries members of the armed forces. When brought in front of the court, a soldier is being court-martialed.

discrimination - unfair treatment based on factors such as a person's race, religion, or gender.

induct - to accept as a member.

integrate - to blend or bring together an organization or society so all members are equal.

letter - the initial of a school awarded to a student for achievement, usually in athletics.

prejudice - hatred of a particular group based on factors such as race or religion.

racism - the belief that one race is better than another.

Web Sites

To learn more about Jackie Robinson, visit ABDO Publishing Company on the World Wide Web at **www.abdopublishing.com.** Web sites about Robinson are featured on our Book Links page. These links are routinely monitored and updated to provide the most current information available.

Index